IDIOT'S GUIDES.
AS EASY AS IT GETS!

P9-DGW-054

Dog Training

by Liz Palika

ALPHA

A member of Penguin Group (USA) Inc.

ALPHA BOOKS

Published by Penguin Group (USA) Inc.

Penguin Group (USA) Inc., 375 Hudson Street, New York, New York 10014, USA • Penguin Group (Canada), 90 Eglinton Avenue East, Suite 700, Toronto, Ontario M4P 2Y3, Canada (a division of Pearson Penguin Canada Inc.) • Penguin Books Ltd., 80 Strand, London WC2R 0RL, England • Penguin Ireland, 25 St. Stephen's Green, Dublin 2, Ireland (a division of Penguin Books Ltd.) • Penguin Group (Australia), 250 Camberwell Road, Camberwell, Victoria 3124, Australia (a division of Pearson Australia Group Pty. Ltd.) • Penguin Books India Pvt. Ltd., 11 Community Centre, Panchsheel Park, New Delhi—110 017, India • Penguin Group (NZ), 67 Apollo Drive, Rosedale, North Shore, Auckland 1311, New Zealand (a division of Pearson New Zealand Ltd.) • Penguin Books (South Africa) (Pty.) Ltd., 24 Sturdee Avenue, Rosebank, Johannesburg 2196, South Africa • Penguin Books Ltd., Registered Offices: 80 Strand, London WC2R 0RL, England

International Standard Book Number: 978-1-61564-418-6
Library of Congress Catalog Card Number: 2013935161

15 14 13   8 7 6 5 4 3 2 1

Interpretation of the printing code: The rightmost number of the first series of numbers is the year of the book's printing; the rightmost number of the second series of numbers is the number of the book's printing. For example, a printing code of 13-1 shows that the first printing occurred in 2013.

Note: This publication contains the opinions and ideas of its author. It is intended to provide helpful and informative material on the subject matter covered. It is sold with the understanding that the author and publisher are not engaged in rendering professional services in the book. If the reader requires personal assistance or advice, a competent professional should be consulted. The author and publisher specifically disclaim any responsibility for any liability, loss, or risk, personal or otherwise, which is incurred as a consequence, directly or indirectly, of the use and application of any of the contents of this book.

Most Alpha books are available at special quantity discounts for bulk purchases for sales promotions, premiums, fund-raising, or educational use. Special books, or book excerpts, can also be created to fit specific needs. For details, write: Special Markets, Alpha Books, 375 Hudson Street, New York, NY 10014.

Trademarks: All terms mentioned in this book that are known to be or are suspected of being trademarks or service marks have been appropriately capitalized. Alpha Books and Penguin Group (USA) Inc. cannot attest to the accuracy of this information. Use of a term in this book should not be regarded as affecting the validity of any trademark or service mark.

Publisher: Mike Sanders

Executive Managing Editor: Billy Fields

Acquisitions Editor: Lori Cates Hand

Development Editor: Megan Douglass

Production Editor: Jana M. Stefanciosa

Photographer: Melissa Duffy

Book Designer/Layout: William Thomas

Indexer: Johnna VanHoose Dinse

Proofreader: Virginia Vought

ALWAYS LEARNING   PEARSON

Contents

Part 4: Training Challenges

Chapter 15: Preventing Problem Behaviors

Chapter 17: Trick Training and Games

Chapter 18: Canine Sports and Activities

Introduction

I was introduced to dog training a number of years ago when my first dog, a German shepherd named Watachie, destroyed my sofa while I was at work one day. And I mean he destroyed it—totally! After cleaning up the mess, I called a local dog trainer and our new journey began.

Since Watachie created that mess in my living room, my dogs and I have trained and/or competed in many dog sports including agility, Canine Good Citizen, carting, conformation, flyball, Frisbee competitions, herding, obedience competitions, schutzhund, search and rescue, therapy dog volunteer work, and weight pulling. Not all at the same time, though, of course.

My joy in teaching Watachie also introduced me to the joys of teaching other dogs and their owners. After an intense education in dogs, dog behavior, and adult education, I began teaching dog training classes. I love to see the understanding between a dog and owner blossom and communication increase.

In This Book

Every dog trainer has his or her own way of training students and their dogs. In this book, I'll share my techniques with you, beginning with an understanding of what training is and how to set some training goals. I use a positive training technique—lure and reward—that will be easy for you to learn and use. We'll also take a look at the importance of the relationship between you and your dog, and how to build that relationship.

Your dog's actions are affected by many things, including what happens in your home and yard, his schedule and yours, and even what goes on in your neighborhood. Sirens make many dogs bark, for example. If you have a highway nearby that fire trucks traverse frequently, and if you have a neighbor who hates barking dogs, there's going to be a problem.

The basic obedience exercises are demonstrated, and in some cases an alternative technique is also provided. Alternative techniques are important because your dog is unique—just like you are.

Common behavior problems are addressed, too, and we'll take a look at things that cause them. Exercise, nutrition, play, and more can all be a part of the solution. Individual problems are addressed with suggested changes you can introduce to correct the problem.

The Photos

Step-by-step instructions are accompanied by photographs detailing each step of the training process to create an easier learning environment for you, the dog owner, If there are any questions in your mind regarding how to interpret the text, you can look to the photos for clarification.

A variety of dogs, breeds, and mixes were used in the photos. I certainly don't want you to feel that only certain dogs or breeds are capable of being trained—that isn't true. Any dog can be trained. If your breed isn't represented in the photos, please don't take offense—we just weren't able to attract one to the photo shoots.

Part 1

Your Relationship with Your Dog

Successful dog training requires a relationship with your dog. The two of you need to care about each other and develop a bond.

Where your dog lives, where he spends his nights, and his normal daily routine affect his behavior. If you're raising a puppy—which includes housetraining—a schedule that works for both you and your puppy is vitally important.

Every dog is an individual, and who your dog is needs to be taken into consideration as you begin training. His breed heritage, temperament, personality, socialization, and past experiences all combine to create your wonderful, unique canine.

Chapter 1

Building a Relationship with Your Dog

- A relationship with your dog is important
- Bonding with your dog
- Think like a parent
- Parents are teachers and leaders

One of the joys of sharing our lives with dogs is the relationship we have with them. Dogs make us laugh, reminding us to play and making sure we play more. Dogs also provide companionship. The bright eyes, wiggling body, and wagging tail of a happy dog can help alleviate sadness and loneliness. We also feel more secure when we live with a dog because the dog's senses are so much better than ours.

No matter whether your canine is a young puppy or a newly adopted adult dog, bonding with the dog is important. The bond that dogs and people share is the foundation for your long-term relationship, and is mutually beneficial to you and your dog. Although it is possible to train a dog without having a relationship with him, it is much harder and significantly less rewarding for both the dog and the trainer. Therefore, concentrating on your relationship with your dog is the first step in beginning a training program.

As your relationship develops, it's important to make sure you are assuming the role of a parent. As a kind, caring parent you will guide and teach your dog so he can be the best he can be. At the same time, your dog learns to look to you for affection, security, and guidance.

Throughout all of this, make sure you take the time to have fun. Play with your dog, talk to him, make silly faces and laugh with him. Throw the ball for him to retrieve, and go to the beach and laugh while he jumps in the waves. Make snowballs and throw them. Cheer for him when he finds the snowball. Having fun is good for your relationship with your dog but also keeps the training from getting too serious.

The Bond Between Dogs and People

It's difficult to explain the bond that develops between dogs and their owners, primarily because it's a feeling. Dog owners who are bonded with their dogs just know it instinctively, while people who have never felt that bond don't understand.

The bond is real, though, and confirmed by science. It is aided by the hormone oxytocin, the same hormone that helps mothers bond with their offspring. Oxytocin also dampens the "fight or flight" instinct so we and our dogs—members of two different species—can have a relationship. No matter how it happens, the bond between dogs and their owners is a wonderful thing and the foundation of a great relationship.

Benefits of the Bond

The benefits of the bond are many. Research has shown that petting a dog will help lower blood pressure and that heart attack patients who have a dog at home have a higher survival rate than those who don't. Dog owners tend to walk their dogs, so they get exercise they might not otherwise get. Dogs help their owners socially, too, because people like to talk about dogs. In short, bonding with a dog provides people with emotional, psychological, and physical benefits.

But dogs gain from this relationship, too. A dog who is bonded to his owner will be happy and feel safe. He will be part of a family. Even though this isn't exactly the same as a wild canine's pack, it does provide emotional and physical security.

A dog who is bonded with his owner, and has participated in training with his owner, will be a happy dog. With training, the dog knows exactly what is expected of him and that provides security. He will have also learned to look to his owner for guidance as to what to do or not do, and what is safe or dangerous.

Bonding with a Puppy

Spending Time Together

The most important aspect of bonding with a puppy is spending time together. This is the easiest way to get to know each other. Let him spend time with you while you're reading, watching television, sitting in front of the computer, or just enjoying some quiet time.

Play with Your Puppy

Playing with your puppy is an integral part of the bonding process because it's fun for both of you. Play retrieving games or tug of war. Tickle your puppy's tummy. The most important thing is to have fun.

Train Your Puppy

Training teaches the puppy there are rules to life with people. At the same time, the puppy and owner are learning how to work together. Not only does this help the bonding process, but the two of you also learn to communicate.

Touch Your Puppy

Giving your puppy a gentle massage each day provides you with a chance to recognize any injuries or potential health problems. At the same time, your puppy learns to trust you as you touch him all over with gentle hands.

Bonding With an Adopted Adult

Take It Slow

Many newly adopted dogs are worried about their situation. They don't know where they are or who you are. Don't try to force your new dog to love you; instead, take it slow and let your dog get to know you.

Keep Him Close

Use the leash to keep your dog close to you at different times throughout the day. He can follow you around as you do chores in the house or outside. While following you and watching you, he is also getting used to you and his new environment.

Begin Training

Training is easier once you and your dog have bonded—but at the same time, the process of training can help develop the bond. Begin training your newly adopted dog. Just be patient, take things slow, and keep the process light and fun.

Walk Your Dog

Walking your dog is a great way to get to know him. You'll learn how he reacts to other people and dogs. In addition, you are introducing him to the world he'll be living in with you. While walking, you're spending time with each other.

Don't Forget to Play

Playing with an adult dog is just as important to the bonding process as it is for a puppy. Play some retrieving games in the house if you can as well as outside. Cheer him on when he brings the toy back.

Touch Him Often

Many newly adopted dogs don't trust strange people. Although new owners feel this means the dog was abused, that's not always true. The dog may simply be cautious around strangers. Touch your dog gently, yet often. Let him learn to trust you.

You will know you and your dog are bonded when you look at him and smile and your dog wags his tail when he sees your smile.

Rules Help Build a Relationship

Many people think that rules for behavior are more associated with punishment than with something positive like building the relationship between you and your dog. But rules and guidelines are important—your dog feels more secure when he has rules to follow—and this can go a long way to helping cement your relationship.

Not a Boss but a Parent

It's important to think of yourself as more of a parent figure for your dog than a boss. Although many bosses are nice people, far too many people think of a boss as a dictator.

However the word *parent* comes with a much different feeling. You don't want to order your dog around like a boss. Instead you want to guide him and teach him. You want to show him what is expected of him. You want to keep him safe. That's what a parent does.

Some people don't like being thought of as a dog's parent. Keep in mind it's the *idea* of parenting that's most important. If you think of yourself as your dog's leader and guardian, you're doing it right.

Parents Are Leaders

A good leader doesn't just tell her followers what to do; she shows them what to do and how it should be done. As your dog's parent, it's important that you do this, too.

Your dog is always learning from you. Some of the lessons are great: if you pause before walking through a doorway, your dog will be more apt to do the same thing as you begin training him. If you're calm when the noisy and potentially scary garbage truck comes down the street, your dog will be calmer as well.

To be a good leader, pay attention to your own behavior and how your dog reacts to it. You may find that you're teaching your dog some things you really didn't want him to know.

Parents Are Protectors

Using the Training

As you train your dog, you can teach behaviors to help keep him safe. By teaching him to sit at open doors and gates, for example, you can protect him from getting hit by a car or becoming lost should he dash out.

Keep You Both Safe

Some rules will help keep both you and your dog safe. For example, teach your dog not to come into the kitchen while you are cooking. By keeping him out from underfoot, you won't trip over him, fall, or drop a hot pan. Look at your home and decide what else you can teach him to keep you both safe.

Safe from Himself

Your dog isn't going to know that some of the things he wants to do could cause him harm. For example, he doesn't understand that moving cars can be deadly. As your dog's parent, you can teach him what you want him to do and prevent the behaviors that could get him hurt.

Dangers Are Many

There are many things in this world that can hurt your dog. You're going to protect him from those dangers as a matter of course; after all, you don't want him to get hurt. Your dog has no idea that you're protecting him, but you are and it will strengthen your bond to your dog.

Parents Are Teachers

The Basic Obedience Exercises

The basic obedience exercises are the foundation for everything else you teach your dog. All dogs deserve a good education in these exercises because they open the lines of communication between you and your dog.

Household Rules

Teaching your dog the rules for living with people is a kindness. Without guidance from you, he'll never understand why raiding a trash can is dangerous or stealing the cat's food is wrong. Teach him the household rules you want him to follow, and he'll be more comfortable in your home.

Public Manners

All dogs need to know how to behave out in public, too. You should be able to greet a neighbor without your dog jumping on her, wrapping the leash around her legs, or barking madly at her. Public manners make life nicer for all concerned.

The Simplest Things

Sometimes it's the simplest things that make the biggest difference. When you teach your dog to lie down and stay at your feet while you're relaxing, you give yourself some peace and quiet while also teaching your dog self-control.

Your Relationship Needs Fun

Although bonding with your dog, building a good relationship, and establishing rules are important, don't forget that you should also be having fun with your dog. Many dog owners put so much pressure on themselves to do everything right that they forget that having fun is one of the primary reasons they added a dog to the family.

Keep the Training Upbeat

You can make the training fun by using it often in different situations rather than always practicing the skills in drills. In addition, be a cheerleader for your dog. When he accomplishes something, praise him: "Yeah! Good boy! You're the smartest dog in the world!" Teach some tricks as you teach the basic exercises. Trick training is great fun and you'll be more likely to laugh with your dog. No matter how you do your training just remember to keep it fun for yourself and your dog.

Don't Get Discouraged

As you begin training your dog, you may find that he'll enjoy the extra attention. But as the training continues, he may act like the old way of doing things was better—that he's really not into this new stuff.

Training is not always a smooth, easy process. If you and your dog are having a tough time, back up—refresh the basic skills again or the first training steps, and then continue on. Don't get angry or frustrated. That will be counterproductive. Not only will it not help the training process, but you can damage your relationship with your dog.

Go slowly, smile, and enjoy the time with your dog as well as the training process. If you find yourself getting frustrated, stop for a while and do something else. Come back to the training when you're calm.

Don't Forget to Play

Play stimulates the mind as well as the body. It causes the body to release stress-relieving hormones. It helps cement your relationship with your dog.

What kind of play you participate in with your dog isn't really important. What *is* important is that both of you enjoy the games, you both have fun, and you laugh with your dog.

Chapter 2

Your Dog's Environment and Training

- The importance of environment
- Environmental stresses
- Help your dog adapt
- Other people can create difficulties

Whether you live in a house or an apartment, in a quiet neighborhood or a noisy one, in the city or the countryside—all of these can affect your dog and her behavior. For example, a retired racing greyhound might be happy in an apartment in the city; many are. But an active young Jack Russell terrier could be bored and destructive in the same situation. Because of the environmental distractions, training alone might not succeed at changing her behavior.

The people in your family or household can also affect your dog's behavior. How many people are in your household? Do they all like your dog? Is normal time with the family quiet and relaxed, or is your family noisy, busy, and rowdy? All of these things can affect your dog's behavior and reactions to training.

Dogs are not solitary creatures. A dog who spends many hours alone each day can develop some behavior problems. However, if someone can alleviate your dog's boredom or loneliness by spending time with her, playing, or taking her for a walk, that would make a difference in her overall behavior and trainability.

Other environmental impacts include both your daily schedule and your dog's—when you leave for work and come home; when the kids come home; when the dog is fed, played with, and goes to bed. Dogs thrive on a schedule; they like it when things happen on time.

Thankfully, dogs are adaptable and can cope with a variety of different living situations and schedules. Just be aware that where and how your dog lives can affect her behavior. Changes that occur around the dog can also cause changes in her behavior.

Your Dog's Living Environment

Dogs have adapted to a variety of living situations. Although many people think of the perfect home for a dog as a suburban home on a tree-lined street with a fenced-in backyard, dogs can also live in condos, apartments, and any other place where people live. That suburban home may be perfect for many dogs; however, as a general rule, dogs are happiest with their people—no matter where they live.

House or Apartment?

That suburban house with a fenced-in yard is perfect for most dogs. The fence can keep her safely secured in the yard and will provide room for the dog to run and play. Greater distances between your home and those of your neighbors help keep complaints about barking to a minimum.

An apartment or condominium can be a different story. Although some apartment and condo developments do allow dogs, many have limitations. Some will limit you to one dog per family or allow dogs only under a certain size or weight.

Without a yard, an apartment dog will need to be walked numerous times a day so she can relieve herself. If that's not possible and you have a very small dog, you may want to housetrain her to a doggy litter box. Without frequent walks or access to a litter box, your dog may develop house-training problems.

People and their dogs can live in other situations—duplexes, military housing, condominiums, mobile homes, a farm house—and dogs can adapt to all of them. However, each will also provide a unique challenge to the dog and dog owner.

City or Country, Quiet or Noisy?

What kind of neighborhood you live in does affect your dog's behavior, and by extension, her training. Dogs can be disturbed by loud music, kids playing, and excited conversations in neighboring backyards. Joggers running past the dog's yard, skateboarders, and bicyclists are stimulating to dogs. Barking dogs in neighboring yards can also keep your dog on edge.

A neighbor who doesn't like dogs can make life unbearable. An angry (or fearful) neighbor could yell at your dog, throw things, squirt her with water from the hose, and who knows what else. Keep the lines of communication open with your neighbors so they know you are training your dog. That way, you can find out if there's a problem before it escalates.

Many people think cities are noisy and rural communities are quiet. Although this can be true, rural communities can have a lot of distractions, too. The sight and smell of livestock can be stimulating to dogs. Large farm vehicles can be loud and often produce smelly exhaust.

Although a neighborhood with a lot going on can cause your dog to bark, dash back and forth inside the fence, or watch carefully out the front window, that doesn't necessarily mean an absolutely quiet community is the best either. If things are normally calm and quiet, your dog may not develop good coping skills. If she's used to no stimulation at all, when exposed to sirens, barking dogs, and other things, she may become fearful or over-excited. She might not know what to do.

Just as no living situation is perfect, neither is any particular neighborhood necessarily better or worse. There are problems and benefits in any situation. As you get ready to begin training, understand that these things can affect your dog's behavior and, as a result, her training.

What Is Nearby?

A school located close to your home can be distracting. The kids walking by every morning and afternoon could cause your dog to bark, run back and forth along the fence of your yard, or jump up at the window or door from inside. A child who regularly teases your dog could create aggression issues in her. A shopping center, bus stop, fire station, or police station could create the same problems.

Dog owners can become so used to their neighborhood that they forget about or just ignore things that dogs pay attention to. If your dog has some bad behaviors that you'd like to change, if you have received complaints from neighbors, or if your dog is suddenly showing some new behaviors, take a fresh look at your neighborhood before you begin training.

Family, Guests, and Other Pets

Everyone who lives with or visits your dog can potentially influence her behavior. People who are calm and cooperate with your training efforts will have a positive impact on your dog. However, people who get your dog excited and those who disregard your training efforts will not help you or your dog at all.

In fact, too many disruptions will confuse your dog. Dogs repeat behaviors that are rewarding, so if your family member encourages the dog to jump up on him and has fun with the dog when he does, the dog will continue jumping. Even if you're trying to teach the dog not to jump, that sporadic reward from the other person will make sure your dog continues to jump up.

Other animals in your home can also affect your dog's behavior. Dogs with a high prey drive (those who like to chase and catch other animals) will be distracted by small animals. Family members paying attention to these small animals can distract your dog, too; jealousy is an emotion that dogs and people share.

All of these scenarios can cause changes in your dog's behavior. These in turn can create a need for basic obedience training or can subvert your training. In other words, these relationships are a part of life that can make things complicated.

People and Pets

Adults in the Home

Ideally, all the adults should agree that the dog needs training and how the training should be accomplished. If someone disagrees and either subverts the training efforts or ignores them, the dog will be confused.

Guests to the Home

Guests rarely have any motivation to help your dog behave himself. Instead, guests are like grandparents who spoil the kids and then send them back to the parents. It's up to you to teach your dog how to behave and interrupt guests who want to spoil your dog.

Children

Children can be great play-mates for dogs. They love to run and chase with the dog or throw the ball. Few kids are interested in training; however, if you can get your kids involved (with your supervision), your dog will end up better behaved with the kids, too.

Another Dog

An older, well-trained dog can be a great help as you train. After all, young dogs naturally imitate behaviors. If your older dog is well behaved and is rewarded for those behaviors, your younger dog will copy him so she can be rewarded, too.

Cats

Dogs and cats don't have to fight like, well, cats and dogs. They can be friends. But dogs love to chase cats when they run, and that can cause a lot of problems. Even a smaller dog can hurt the cat—and a large dog could kill the cat. Training can teach your dog that chasing is not allowed.

Other Pets

Even though they have been domesticated for thousands of years, dogs are predators. Some dogs get along fine with smaller pets, but many dogs will enjoy chasing and catching small pets. Training can help teach the dog self-control. Still, you should supervise the dog's interactions with these pets.

Dogs who show a strong prey drive—chasing birds and squirrels—should not be allowed to interact with smaller, caged pets at all.

Your Dog's Daily Routine

Time Alone

Dogs are not solitary creatures; they are descended from animals that lived in family groups. A dog who spends many hours alone can develop behavior problems that may include barking, self-mutilation, destructive chewing, digging, and much more.

The Daytime Hours

Your dog would be happiest if she could spend her day with you. If your dog needs to be left home alone, where does she stay? Where would she be happiest? Is she able to get outside? Your routine is unique, so choose something that will work for both of you.

Quiet Time

At some point during your day, share some quiet time with your dog. You can do this in the living room, out on your patio, or at the local coffee shop's patio. It's important for your dog to understand that not all your time together is active; you can be relaxed together, too.

Time for Exercise

A dog who doesn't get enough exercise will be prone to get into trouble. Make sure your dog's daily routine includes a chance to run or play some retrieving games, whether in your backyard or at a local park.

Training Time

Make sure your dog's daily routine includes some time spent training. It doesn't need to be a big chunk of time—5 minutes before you feed her breakfast, 5 minutes during your lunch break, 5 minutes when you get home, and 5 minutes later in the evening is great.

Where Does She Sleep?

Although a well-trained adult dog can sleep on your bed or have free run of the house, your puppy, newly adopted dog, or any dog in training should sleep in her crate. This gives your dog her own space and will prevent problem behaviors from developing.

The Importance of a Schedule

Dogs thrive on a schedule. Most puppy owners understand that puppies need a schedule if they are to be reliably housetrained. But adult dogs are also happier when their lives have a routine. When the important things in your dog's life happen at certain times, your dog will feel secure and comfortable.

Events that should happen at regular times each day may include the following:

- **Meals:** Puppies need to eat three to four times a day, depending on your veterinarian's recommendations. Most adult dogs do well on two meals a day: one in the morning and one in the evening. Housetraining skills develop better—and remain good—when meals happen at regular times each day.

- **Housetraining trips outside:** These, too, should happen at regular intervals, depending on the dog's needs. Puppies need to relieve themselves often throughout the waking hours, while adult dogs can go outside less often. A schedule prevents housetraining accidents.

- **Exercise and playtime:** Although it's not as important for exercise to happen on schedule as it is for meals or trips outside, keeping on a schedule gives dogs something to look forward to—and they do exactly that.

- **Walks:** Dogs may not be able to tell time on a clock, but they know when it's time to go for a walk. Your dog may sit in front of the door waiting for you to get ready, or she may get her leash and bring it to you. Because your dog's walk is important to her, it should also be on a schedule.

- **Sleep:** Dogs need regular sleep just as people do. Ideally, she should go to bed and get up at relatively the same times each day.

Your schedule may vary sometimes and it may be difficult to follow the schedule, but these suggestions are the ideal. Dogs are adaptable and will be able to cope with some changes. The house-training schedule, however, needs to be followed as closely as possible because once a dog begins relieving herself in the house, that habit can be hard to change.

Be Aware

Now that you know that your dog's environment can affect her behavior and your training efforts, pay attention to it. Many behavior problems pop up when the dog's environment changes.

For example, when the kids have been home from school for the summer and then go back to school in the fall, that constitutes a major change in the dog's environment. Her playmates are gone all day now and she may react by barking, chewing up the kids' toys, or hiding in the kids' rooms.

If you see a change in your dog's behavior, take a look at what's happening around her. After you identify the problem, you can work to change it.

Chapter 3

Who Is Your Dog?

- The breed's original job
- Gender can affect behavior
- Temperament and personality
- Socialization is vital

Who your dog is makes a big difference in how you approach his training, how he accepts and cooperates with the training, and even how well he retains what he has been taught. These can all be affected by the various characteristics that make your dog who he is.

If asked who your dog is, you would probably answer with your dog's name and his pertinent details: "My dog is Buddy, a golden retriever." This is true; most people think of a particular dog's breed when they first see him. When you go for a walk do people greet you and your dog, "Oh, I love golden retrievers! May I pet him?" Or do they say, "Golden retrievers are so rowdy and silly! Why would you ever have one?" Even though these are generalizations, each breed does have some individual attributes and these do need to be considered when training your dog.

Purebred dogs are not the only dogs with breed characteristics; mixed breed dogs have attributes from the various dogs in their ancestry. If your dog is the result of a breeding of two purebred dogs, then discovering the breed heritage is easier. But if your dog is the result of generations of mixed breeds, then figuring out his heritage will be significantly more difficult, if not impossible.

Your dog is much more than just his breed or mixture of breeds. Your dog's age makes a difference to training, as does whether he (or she) is male, female, neutered, or spayed. Your dog's past experiences, including the socialization he's had, also play a big part in how he reacts to training.

Your dog's temperament and personality also play a big part in how you will approach his training. If he's reserved and calm but a little shy, for example, you will need to make sure you aren't too boisterous, loud, pushy, or demanding with your training. You will have to take your time and let him absorb each lesson before you move on to the next one.

Training isn't limited only to those dogs who are purebreds, the easiest to train, or the most receptive to training. Every dog deserves a chance to learn. Keep in mind, too, that the training isn't going to change who your dog is. Instead, training will help cement your relationship and will make him a better friend to have around.

Heritage Affects Behavior

Most people know that Border collies are great sheep herding dogs, German shepherds are often used for police work, and Labrador retrievers are one of the most commonly used breeds for service dog work. These breeds have done these jobs so often that they have become recognizable in these positions.

What most people don't realize is that wise breeders have bred their dogs so the characteristics that allow these dogs to do their jobs so capably are present in their offspring. Dogs who are not able to do the job are not used for breeding. These traits, then, become that breed's heritage—breed traits that are passed from parents to their offspring.

More than 400 canine breeds are recognized all over the world. Most have been created for a certain purpose. Some help people move livestock while others protect livestock from

predators. Some dog breeds were bred to protect property, others to protect their owners, while others have no protective instincts at all and were instead bred for friendliness. The jobs that dogs can do for mankind are various and many.

Each of these occupations requires certain skills. The dachshund that hunted badgers needed to be able to go down tunnels, so a flexible body and short but strong legs helped. The dog also needed to be fearless, and most dachshunds show these traits.

Training can accomplish many things but it cannot change who the dog is. Understanding your dog's breed, what it was originally designed to do, and how those characteristics helped the dog do his job will aid you as you begin training your dog.

Your Dog's Details

Your dog's breed heritage isn't the only attribute of his that will affect how you train him and how well he learns. Anything that makes your dog who he is must be taken into consideration.

How Old Is Your Dog?

Dogs of any age can be taught and are capable of learning. But not all dogs learn the same way. Sometimes the training method needs to be adapted to better serve a particular dog.

Puppies can start learning as soon as they join their new family. Most puppies go home at 8 to 10 weeks of age, and at this age their brains are fully functional and ready to learn. Housetraining, social skills, and easy obedience exercises can all be introduced.

There are two things that must be taken into account when teaching your puppy. The first is that puppies of this age are babies and the training must be gentle. Emphasize showing the puppy what to do rather than interrupting mistakes. In addition, puppies are easily distracted. Their concentration isn't good right now, so limit training sessions to just a couple minutes at a time and keep it fun.

Puppies turn into adolescents (teenagers) anywhere between 7 and 10 months of age, with 9 months being the most common. In adolescence, your puppy may become more challenging, which often makes training difficult. At this age, it's important to build motivation so your teenager wants to cooperate with you. Don't fight with him—trying to force him to work with you—as this will be counterproductive.

Adult dogs are ready and willing to learn. They may have some bad habits that have already been learned, but training can help change those. Older adults, even geriatric dogs, can still learn. The adage, "You can't teach an old dog new tricks," is false. You will have to take into consideration your older dog's physical ailments, if he has any, when training him—but other than that, have fun.

His Previous Experiences

Everything that has happened to your dog throughout his life has influenced who he is today. If he is a young puppy, you're not dealing with much, just his experiences with his breeder and with you. Hopefully his experiences were kind and gentle yet mentally stimulating.

An adult dog who has grown up without any training—and especially one who has been spoiled or allowed to do just about anything he wants to do—may not readily take to the training. After all, life was good, so why change it? But he can learn new things and when he does, you can change some of his undesirable habits and create new ones.

If you have adopted an adult dog, everything that has happened to him at his previous homes, at the shelter or rescue, and at your home is now a part of him. Unfortunately, with a newly adopted dog, there will be a lot you don't know and this can be a challenge.

For example, if the dog has been hit with an object—let's say a broom—you won't know that until you try to sweep the floor. When your dog rolls over to bare his belly, runs from the room, or attacks the broom, you'll realize something horrible has happened that included a broom.

These unknown experiences can create some difficulties in both your life with your dog and your training. You'll just have to pay attention, watch your dog's reactions, and deal with the issues as they appear.

Male Characteristics

As a general rule, male dogs are larger than females in their breed—taller, broader, and stronger. Males are loyal, dedicated, and watchful.

Some male puppies will mount toys, the family cat, other dogs, or even a person's leg, and while doing this, will move the hips in a simulated sexual act. Contrary to common belief, this is not—in puppyhood—a sexual act. Nor is it necessarily an act of dominance. However, we don't consider it socially acceptable, so feel free to interrupt your puppy to stop the behavior.

Male dogs also lift a rear leg to urinate on vertical surfaces to mark territory. This is saying to other dogs, "Hi. I've been here and I can pee this high on this post." This is okay if the dog does it once or twice on a walk, but if the dog tries to mark multiple vertical objects, then it's becoming a problem. Dogs who mark in the house have a bad habit, too, especially if they mark guests' belongings. Training can help you control this issue.

Many male dogs are neutered (castrated) once they reach adolescence. It has been recommended to help prevent a canine overpopulation problem and to prevent male sexual behaviors, especially mounting, excessive leg lifting, and escaping from the yard.

But because there are some risks associated with neutering male dogs, it is not always necessary—especially if your dog is not showing any sexually-related bad behaviors. Talk to your veterinarian about the pros and cons of neutering and make an informed decision.

Neutering the male dog doesn't change who he is. It simply removes the sexual hormones and desires. He will otherwise be the same dog he was before the surgery.

Female Characteristics

Female dogs do not have as many sexually related bad behaviors as males can have. Some females will mount other dogs, but this usually occurs only when the female is in season and is ready to be bred. Some may also lift their leg to urinate but it's not that common.

Spaying the female is usually done to prevent an unwanted pregnancy. It can also be done as a convenience because a female dog in season can be messy. She will also attract all the male dogs in the neighborhood; you may find one or more unknown male dogs hanging around your yard when she's in season.

As with the males, however, talk to your veterinarian and find out the pros and cons of spaying. Ask about any side effects or potential problems and then make a decision.

Temperament, Personality, and Socialization

Your dog's temperament and personality are what defines who he is mentally (as opposed to his physical conformation). The combination of these traits is what makes every dog unique.

Socialization is also a part of the dog's mental makeup. Socialization must begin in early puppyhood, but it needs to continue throughout the dog's lifetime. A lack of socialization can create some serious problems.

Temperament Is Present at Birth

Your dog is born with his own temperament. His temperament is his nature—his way of feeling and reacting. Breed traits are a large part of temperament, although every dog—even dogs within the same breed—will also have his own individual characteristics.

Most temperament traits are passed down from parents and grandparents. If your dog's parents are watchful and protective, or silly and playful, then your dog will be more apt to have those traits, too.

These traits make your dog who he is and therefore must be taken into consideration when you begin training him. A playful dog can be motivated to cooperate with training by using a favorite toy or ball as a reward. If you know you have a dog who tends to be stubborn, you should avoid pushing him to do what you want and instead use food treats, play, or other motivators so he decides to cooperate on his own.

Personalities Are Unique

Temperament and personality are closely related; after all, they both help to create who your dog is. But whereas your dog's temperament was present at birth, his personality is affected by what happens to him during his life.

A dog who was born with a happy, playful temperament can change if he isn't well socialized as a puppy, is neglected, or is treated badly. Instead of going through life happy and playful, he may become fearful and cautious.

Training, too, can affect a dog's personality. If the training process is structured, predictable, and fun, the dog will retain (or gain) a more positive outlook and will be cooperative with your training efforts. This positive outlook can spread to other parts of his life including playtime, going for a walk, and even visiting the veterinarian.

However, if the dog dislikes your training efforts, or if the training is overly rough, then his personality can suffer. He may have a less than positive outlook on life and may fight your efforts to teach him.

Is Your Dog Well Socialized?

Socialization is the process of introducing your dog to the world around him. Ideally, this should begin when puppies are between 12 and 16 weeks of age. This is when puppies are ready to learn what their world is all about. They should see, smell, hear, and touch new things—including people, other puppies, and friendly dogs—and have fun doing it.

This stage of life is so critical that if it doesn't happen during puppyhood it is difficult (and sometimes impossible) to do later in life. A dog who hasn't been well socialized in puppyhood might be fearful of new things, can overreact, or may be aggressive when faced with something or someone new.

Your dog's socialization experiences are definitely a part of his personality. His confidence (or lack of confidence) in himself and in you is based on his ability to handle new and unexpected things—all based on his socialization as a puppy.

If your dog is past puppyhood, don't think he can be isolated at home. He still needs to get out into the world. Although he's past the age of socialization, he needs the stimulation of going places and doing things. An isolated dog will be less able to cope with new things and experiences.

Part 2

Explaining Dog Training

What are your goals for training your dog? It's a good idea to know what you want to accomplish—at least in part—so you can work toward those goals. You can always amend or add on to your goals as you progress through the training process. A well-trained dog is a joy, so don't be afraid to have some high expectations.

A lure and reward training technique is positive, easy to use, and makes training enjoyable for your dog. Plus, it's easy for dog owners to learn and use. Training is not difficult. Just follow the step-by-step instructions, be patient, and strive to make it fun for both you and your dog.

Chapter 4

Set Training Goals

- Good behavior has benefits
- What would you like?
- Your dog is capable of a lot
- List some goals

Many dog owners don't have any expectations for their dogs at all. If the dog chews on shoes or digs up the backyard, well, that's just what dogs do. When their dog jumps on guests, dashes out an open door, or barks at people from the car, the excuses are many but nothing is done to change those behaviors.

Dogs are capable of so much more. For most of our history with dogs, mankind wasn't rich enough to keep animals that didn't serve a function. Dogs had jobs; they herded livestock or protected it. They pulled carts, guarded people or property, flushed game, retrieved birds, and hunted vermin. Although most dogs today don't perform their ancestral jobs, they can be well behaved; much more so than their owners expect or even understand.

You might feel, as so many other dog owners do, that setting goals for your training program seems like you're setting yourself up to fail. But without goals—and especially without high expectations—you and your dog will never achieve what you both are capable of doing.

You can also set different levels of goals. Teaching your dog the basic obedience exercises can be the first, followed by changing some behavior problems that have bugged you. After that, perhaps some trick training. Maybe you and your dog can work toward passing the Canine Good Citizen test, or you might want to be a certified therapy dog team. After that, what else?

To accomplish anything, though, you must have faith in yourself, in your ability to teach your dog, and in your dog's ability to learn. You both can do this.

Good Behavior Is a Joy

Everyone who shares their home with a dog knows that living with a dog requires some sacrifice. Dirt will be tracked in on the carpets, leaves and sticks will be carried inside, and bodily functions will make an appearance at odd moments. This is all a part of owning a dog.

A dog who has had some training is more fun to live with. A well-behaved dog is a companion rather than simply someone to clean up after or a pain in the neck because she's always causing a problem.

A Well-Behaved Dog Is More Fun

A well-behaved dog is a lot more fun and far less trouble than a dog who isn't trained. With training and some rules for good behavior, your dog can go places and have more fun with you.

The two of you can go for enjoyable walks to local parks, historical sites, and even outside shopping malls. Many regional, county, and state parks allow dogs to go for hikes with their owners. Rules vary according to location, so check them out. But a hike in the forest, meadows, or mountains is great exercise and renews the spirit.

A well-behaved dog will enjoy going on family picnics or get-togethers. Camping trips with the family are wonderful. Your dog can play retrieving games or swim in the ocean or a lake.

If you begin to feel overwhelmed while setting goals and beginning the training process, just think of all you will be able to do with your dog. The end result is worth the effort.

You Won't Be Embarrassed

Far too many dogs stay at home—without going for walks or on outings—because their owners are embarrassed by the dog's behavior. Granted, a dog who pulls too hard on the leash, jumps on people, lunges at other dogs, and urinates on every vertical object is embarrassing. But the dog doesn't have to behave in that manner.

As you're thinking about goals for your dog's behavior, consider the behaviors she has that bother you. Then as you set some goals, you can place changing those behaviors on your list.

Save Some Money

It's amazing how much damage a dog can do—especially one with some bad habits. Chewing up landscaping, digging up the sprinkler system, and destroying the cable into the house for the television and internet can all add up.

The damage in the house can be just as bad. Many dogs have chewed up remotes, eye glasses, shoes, slippers, and even edges of the carpet. Sofa cushions, table legs, edges of wooden furniture, and hearing aids all fall victim to canine destroyers.

All of this damage should never be considered normal behavior. It costs a great deal of money to repair or replace many of the items.

You'll Enjoy Your Dog

A well-behaved dog who isn't constantly causing a problem is fun. You'll enjoy spending time with her. She'll snuggle up with you in the evenings while you watch the news or read a book. She'll just hang out with you while you're doing laundry.

A well-behaved dog can go just about anywhere with you—at least anywhere that dogs are allowed. Take your dog with you when you go to the coffee shop and sit on the outside patio. Most hardware stores welcome well-behaved dogs. Go to an outdoor art show, craft sale, or holiday bazaar and bring your dog with you.

You'll know that your dog truly is a part of the family when you schedule vacations to places where your dog is welcome, too. Vacation will be a lot more fun when your dog is with you because you will be seeing things from her perspective. She'll let you know when the deer are up on the hill across from your campsite or when a kite is flying overhead.

A well-behaved dog is a true companion. She's a friend you really like who makes you feel secure, keeps you company, and makes you laugh.

Have High Expectations

If asked, most dog owners would agree that a well-behaved dog is a joy. However, every dog own-er's definition of a well-behaved dog is different. Some dog owners want a dog who listens to and obeys every command while others don't mind a little bit of defiance. Some owners want their dogs to stay off the furniture while others enjoy snuggling with their dogs. These differences in interpretation are fine; that's why you will establish your own goals.

As you think about goals for the future, don't be afraid to set high expectations. Most dogs are not asked to do anything near what they're capable of, and that's too bad. Dogs are happy when they get a chance to exercise their brains as much as their bodies.

Your Dog Is Capable of So Much

A Border collie in Spartanburg, South Carolina, knows the names of 1,022 individual items. It took his trainers three years to teach Chaser the names of all of these items but he now knows them.

When this hit the news, many people commented that the dog was able to do this only because he is a Border collie and they are known for their intelligence and strong work ethic. Border collies are smart and they do love to work, but many other breeds, mixes, and individual dogs have the same abilities.

There is no reason most dogs can't learn obedience training, trick training, and some dog activities and sports. There is so much dogs can do!

That doesn't mean that a dog should be asked to do something that goes against her nature. Few Jack Russell terriers will be good herding dogs, although it wouldn't be a surprise if one or two have been able to do it. Chances of success are better when the dog is asked to do things she is capable of doing.

Decide What You'd Like

Have you met a dog that you admire? Is a neighbor or friend's dog well trained, polite yet friendly, and a perfect lady out in public? Does that dog behave herself when you go to their home? Does she like to play? Does the family take her places? What is it that you like so much about this dog?

Now, let's think about your dog. What would you like to change or to teach your dog?

- **Household manners:** Perhaps you'd like to teach your dog to behave better in the house. Dashing out open doors, raiding the trash cans, or chewing on household items can all be dangerous as well as annoying. Think about the things you would like to change.

- **Manners with people:** Dogs who jump on people can damage clothes, scratch skin, and even knock people down. Dogs who use their teeth on people's clothing or skin can cause damage, too, and may be accused of biting.

- **Behavior around other dogs:** If your dog pulls you toward other dogs, barks at them, or lunges, he's being rude. Other dogs are apt to respond negatively because these actions aren't polite.

- **What else:** If you had a magic wand, what would you ask for?

When thinking about these goals, don't let people talk you out of your ideas. People will say that certain breeds are smarter than others, that some are dumb, or that your dog will never be able to accomplish anything. Don't listen to these people.

Dream Big

Now that you've had a pep talk and a chance to think about it, what goals would you like to set for yourself, your training program, and your dog? As you establish these, think of them in a positive manner. Although in the last section we talked about bad behaviors and changing them, as you set goals, list them as something to teach rather than to change.

For example, if your dog raids the kitchen trash can, list your goal as, "Prevent Sweetie from getting into the trash can and teach her to ignore it." By thinking of this goal as proactive rather than, "Break Sweetie's horrible habit of raiding the trash can," your chance of success will be much better.

Also, as you create your goals, don't be afraid of dreaming big. You both can do anything you want to do. But here are some suggestions to help get you thinking:

Start with Basic Obedience

All of your future goals begin here. The basic obedience exercises help develop communication between you and your dog and teach your dog self-control. The exercises themselves have many applications.

Your Dog and Your Yard

Your dog and a nicely landscaped yard can coexist. Can you establish an area for your dog where she can relieve herself and not burn your grass? Where do you want her to play? Think about details such as these while setting your goals.

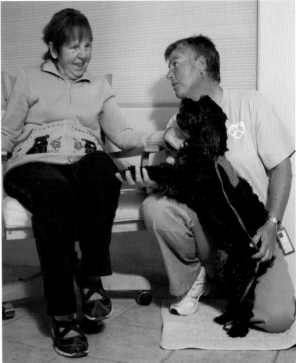

Traveling With Your Dog

Family vacations are more fun when the whole family gets to go, and that includes the dog. It does require some additional planning and logistics, but your dog will add to the adventure. As you think about this as a potential goal, consider whether it will work for the type of vacations you normally take.

Therapy Dog

There are many fun and worthwhile activities available for well-behaved dogs, such as therapy dog volunteer work. Would you like to take your dog to visit people in nursing homes and hospitals? Seeing people smile as they pet your dog will make your day. This requires basic obedience training as well as some specialized training.

Jot Down Your Goals

Once you have decided on some goals for yourself and your dog, jot them down. Put them in order, beginning with basic obedience training, which can be followed by problem prevention and solving. Then decide which goals should follow in what order.

Now post that list where you'll see it often. Put it on the refrigerator, near where you hang your dog's leash, or in your calendar book or online calendar.

Chapter 5

Choose a Training Method

Researchers don't know for sure when dogs joined with mankind to create a mutually beneficial relationship, but estimates range from 15,000 to 33,000 years ago. No matter how long ago this happened, it's not unreasonable to believe that some kind of training began right away.

As the relationship progressed over the years, dogs and people learned to communicate and people found that certain things could cause dogs to change their behavior. As dogs began to help people hunt or protect them from predators, the communication between species improved.

Some of the first known incidences of training were with dogs used to help mankind during wars. In the mid-seventh century B.C.E., horses and dogs were both used by the Magnesian warriors when fighting the Ephesians. The Spanish conquistadors also brought horses and dogs (mastiffs) with them when invading the Americas. The size and ferocity of the mastiffs was intimidating to the native people, but so was the behavior of the well-trained dogs.

Today there are many different ways to train dogs, just as there are many techniques for teaching people. Ideally the training technique you use should be easy for you to understand, comfortable for you to use, and your dog should learn without confusion. That's asking a lot from any technique, but it's certainly possible. A lure and reward technique, as taught in this book, is a positive technique that helps a dog learn the behaviors desired of him, rather than concentrating on what he's doing wrong.

The Basis of Training

The science of dog training is explained by the four quadrants of operant conditioning. All dog training methods can be explained by these four phrases. Although it's not necessary for you to know and understand these, they can help you decide how you want to train your dog.

Positive Reinforcement

Positive reinforcement means you are adding something to the process. You could be giving the dog a treat, petting him, or tossing a tennis ball. These things are rewards for cooperating with you; for doing something that you would like him to continue doing. For example, if you ask your dog to sit and then give him a treat and pet him, the treat and petting are positive reinforcements. Your dog will be more likely to sit in the future to earn those things he likes.

The key for making a positive reinforcement work is that the dog must like it. If a dog is not interested in food or hates having his head petted, then those things aren't going to be considered positive reinforcements. Positive reinforcement is the technique used by most trainers today because it's gentle, kind to dogs, and easy for trainers to use.

Negative Reinforcement

The theory behind negative reinforcement states that something the dog considers aversive is used during bad behavior and then is removed when the dog's behavior changes. To avoid the negative reinforcement the dog no longer performs the unwanted behavior.

For dogs who pull, for example, the owner might say, "No pull!" and give the dog a pop with the leash. The theory says that when the dog reacts and slows down, there is slack in the leash and the dog walks next to the owner.

However, negative reinforcement is rarely effective by itself. For example, for the dog who is pulling on the leash, the dog must first be taught how to walk on a leash nicely without pulling before negative reinforcement will work at all to change the dog's behavior. Otherwise he'll continue to pull on or fight the leash because he doesn't know what to do instead.

Negative **means you're taking something away. You may refuse to give your dog the treat (negative punishment) or release the tension on the leash (negative reinforcement).**

Positive means you're adding something to the process. You could give a treat (positive reinforcement) or a verbal interruption (positive punishment).

Positive Punishment

When positive punishment is used, something the dog dislikes is used to decrease the frequency of a behavior. Although the word punishment is equated with things like yelling, shock collars, or other harsh training techniques, this isn't necessarily so, and unless there are exceptional circumstances and situations, those techniques are to be avoided.

Positive punishment doesn't have to be harsh. If the dog is playing in the house and becomes overstimulated, he could be removed from the area of play until he calms down. Taking him away from the play, or isolating him from playmates or the attention of his owner, are all positive punishments. Many trainers consider certain positive punishments, especially time-outs, to be useful tools when used in a balance with positive reinforcements.

Negative Punishment

Although negative punishment may sound bad, it's an easy-to-use technique that is not harmful when training your dog. With this technique, something rewarding that your dog likes is removed or taken away.

Let's say you have a treat in your hand and you ask your dog to sit. Instead of sitting, he jumps up on you. You take that treat and put it back in your pocket, turn, and walk away. No treat and no attention from you. The next time you ask your dog to sit, he's more apt to sit rather than jump on you.

Your Dog Is the Key

Although these four quadrants of operant conditioning seem workable on paper, your dog is the key to what should be used while training him. Some dogs will work nicely for positive reinforcements only and may never put a paw wrong. Other dogs may need more to help them change bad habits. Experiment to find the right balance for both you and your dog.

Thinking about these four quadrants while actually training your dog isn't at all practical. You aren't going to question yourself about which quadrant to use while your dog is chasing the family cat. You should, however, think about these aspects of training as you plan and begin your training program. Training is a long-term process and you need to be comfortable with it.

A Variety of Training Methods

No one training method is right for all dogs. Not only do dog owner temperaments and personalities differ, but so do dogs. Breed heritages differ, too. A soft, slightly timid toy poodle is not going to cooperate as well with a forceful training method, and in fact will probably be traumatized by this method. Yet that firmer method might suit a bold Rottweiler just fine. It's important to find the method—or combination of methods —that suits both you and your dog.

Lure and Reward

A lure and reward training method is exactly what it sounds like: you will use something the dog likes as a lure (food treats or a toy). Use that to help him do something you want him to do, and then he gets rewarded. The reward is verbal praise first, followed by the lure.

It's important that your voice is the first reward. For example, when he looks at you, "Yes!" can pinpoint (or mark) the behavior you want. It takes a few seconds to get a treat to his mouth but you can say yes instantly. Plus, the treat reward is going to be used during the initial training, but then you are going to phase it out. Verbal praise can remain.

Clicker Training

A clicker—a small mechanism that makes a short, sharp sound—is used to let the dog know he has done something right. In the first steps of the training, the dog learns an association between the click and a food reward.

The hardest part of this method is developing the timing needed to communicate to the dog exactly when he's done the right thing. Many people, especially at first, tend to be one thought behind the dog, "Oh, right, I need to click now." This delay in timing can be confusing to the dog.

The sound of a clicker marks the correct behavior. It is fast and sharp and lets the dog know immediately when he's done something right.

Balanced Training

Balanced training usually refers to a method that uses more than one quadrant of the operant conditioning chart. Balanced training is generally based on teaching dogs what to do and rewarding them for that, but also letting the dogs know when they have made a mistake. This can work, depending on the method of letting the dog know he's made a mistake, and as long as the trainer also then shows the dog what to do instead. Corrections just for the sake of punishing the dog are not considered good dog training and are not effective.

Choosing a Method

It's important that you feel comfortable with the method you use. If you feel that something you're doing is wrong—or that it is confusing your dog—then stop using it. Think about what you've been doing: where is the problem? Where is your dog getting confused? Have you forgotten a step in the training?

Then try again. If you're still having problems you might want to ask a dog trainer for some help. Perhaps she can clear up your confusion. If things still feel wrong, then you may want to try another method.

Why Use Lure and Reward

The exercises in this book are taught using a lure and reward method. This method was chosen because it is a positive method that is kind to the dogs. Plus, because it's easy to learn, most dog owners like it. This method can also be used for many different exercises—from basic obedience to trick training and more.

A lure and reward method is also adaptable. If you would like to try a clicker, it can be added into a lure and reward method without confusion. If you find that your dog needs more than just positive reinforcement, you can also add in one or two techniques from another quadrant to help him learn. A lure and reward method can be molded to fit individual dogs quite easily.

Dogs tend to cooperate with this method because it is easy for them to follow and there is less chance for confusion. Plus, rewards are easy to earn.

Dogs will repeat actions that are rewarding. For example, if the dog raids the kitchen trash can and finds some food scraps in the trash, he will raid the trash can again because finding the food scraps was a reward. This is why a training method that uses rewards can be so effective.

Using a Lure

The idea of using a lure to help your dog move into a certain position or to do something you ask him to do might seem a little overwhelming, but it's really quite easy. In fact, with a little practice it will become second nature.

Just think of the lure as a tiny magnet. The other imaginary magnet is in your dog's nose. You will let the two magnets attach—your thumb and fingers holding the treat in front of your dog's nose—and then move his nose with the treat. You can then help him assume a position or make a movement. This is called *shaping;* you're shaping a behavior.

You can also use the lure to bring the dog to you from a distance. Again, think of the lure as a magnet pulling your dog closer and closer to you.

Choosing a Lure

The lure must be something your dog really likes that he doesn't often get. Remember that saying that familiarity breeds contempt? If the lure is something your dog gets on a regular basis it will not be special enough to use as a lure.

If you choose a food (or foods) to use as a lure, keep in mind that your dog's sense of smell is much stronger than his sense of taste. So Swiss cheese, for example, with its stronger smell, will be a better lure for most dogs than a blander food.

Freeze-dried meats make good lures, as can cooked meats left over from dinner, other strong cheeses, and microwaved slices of hot dogs. Healthy, commercial, meat-based treats are also good lures. Because you will be using quite a few treats in the beginning of training, avoid junk foods or commercial treats that aren't good-quality foods.

Alternating foods can help keep your dog's attention. Using freeze-dried liver one day and Swiss cheese the next will keep your dog guessing and his nose twitching.

If your dog is not motivated by food, choose a toy that is special to your dog. A tennis ball will work for ball addicts. A squeaky toy, especially one with a different-sounding squeaker, can be great. A fuzzy, fluffy stuffed toy might be special enough, too. Do some experimentation to see what will work best.

The lure will be used in most of the exercises that will be taught throughout this book. Here are four exercises to give you a chance to play with the lure and get the feel of how to use it.

How to Lure Your Dog

Close to You

With a lure, you can bring the dog in close to you. This is important, as it's tough to teach your dog if he prefers to remain at arm's length from you. With your dog on leash, let him sniff the treat and back away from him. Don't give him any commands, just use the treat to have him follow you a few steps. Praise him, "Good boy!" and pop the treat in his mouth.

Maneuver your Dog

You can use the lure to help your dog change position. The lure in front of his nose and the movements of your hand, arm, and body will serve as a guide. To practice it right now, let your dog sniff the treat and then move your hand (and his nose) in a circle in front of you so that he's moving in a circle. Praise him and pop the treat in his mouth.

Attention to You

A lure will help you gain your dog's attention. If he's looking away, sniffing, pulling, or otherwise ignoring you, you can't teach him. With your dog on leash, let him sniff the lure. Then move your hand up toward your face. As he looks at you, praise him and pop the treat in his mouth.

Building Excitement

Very few dogs ask to be trained. Once they learn that the training process can be fun, they're more willing to cooperate. Using a lure to help the dog learn and to reward the dog builds excitement about training. Offer the treat and see how excited he can get.

Making the Lure Disappear

The lure is a training tool that you'll use when it's needed—especially when teaching your dog something new. You won't use it forever, however, because you don't want your dog to cooperate with you only when you have a treat.

How Long to Use the Lure

Use the lure long enough for your dog to learn not only the hand signal with the treat but also the verbal cue (or command) that you'll teach with each exercise. When you initially teach your dog something new, he will learn the hand signal first because he'll be paying attention to the treat in your hand. He'll learn the verbal cue second, so make sure you continue using the lure through that learning stage.

However, when your dog will do the exercise when you ask using only the verbal cue, then you can begin weaning him from the lure. Do not simply stop using the lure, because if you do, he will stop cooperating with you. At this point in his training no treat equals no performance.

Make the Lure Intermittent

Once your dog knows a particular exercise, the first step in making the lure disappear is to give it to your dog randomly. Think of a slot machine in Las Vegas; people continue to play the slots because they win at random times. That random reinforcement drives them to play even more. The same applies to your dog.

So, before you fade that lure and treat away completely, make it random:

- Use the treat lure and reward every second or third time you ask the dog to do that particular exercise. But don't give it reliably every second or third time; mix it up. Continue to use verbal praise and petting all the time.

- After a couple of weeks, provide the treat reward only when your dog is doing the exercise particularly well. If he's doing it quickly, with good attention, or in the correct position—depending on the exercise—give him a treat or two. Use the verbal praise and petting all the time.

- When your dog does something particularly well, offer a jackpot of treats—a handful—with lots of verbal praise. Just as a jackpot at the slot machine keeps you playing, a jackpot of treats keeps your dog working for you.

Gradually, decrease the treats but continue giving your dog the verbal praise for his cooperation and efforts. You will continue with that; it's not going away.

When to Bring Back the Lure

There are several instances when it might be necessary to bring back the lure. The first would be if you are going to teach your dog something new. If you decide to do some trick training or teach your dog a new sport, the lure will help you teach the new exercises.

You can bring back the lure if your dog is going through a tough time. Adolescence, for example, is always hard; your puppy's brain is changing and maturing and he'll often be less cooperative than normal. The lure can help gain his attention and motivate him to work with you rather than challenge you.

If you haven't been practicing with your dog's training, and his behavior slips, bringing back the lure can help the two of you polish those skills. Use the lure long enough to reestablish your working relationship and then fade the lure away again.

There are no hard and fast rules as to when to make the lure disappear. Use your intuition and your knowledge of your dog. And then, if his skills slip or he's having trouble, bring the lure back for some refresher training.

Chapter 6

Your Training Tools

- Your voice is the most important tool
- Treats and toys are good motivators
- Collars and leashes aid communication

Although you may think of a tool as something mechanical, in dog training it's anything that helps you teach your dog.

Your most important training tool is your voice. Not only do you always have your voice, your dog is used to hearing it. You may need to learn how to use it most effectively, but once you know how, it's a great dog training tool.

Anything that will help you motivate your dog to cooperate with your training efforts can be a training tool. Food treats work for many dogs, but some will do better with toys that squeak or tennis balls. Every dog is unique, so part of the process is finding what will motivate your dog.

It's important to choose the right tools for you and your dog, and then use them long enough to get to know them. Changing tools frequently may confuse both you and your dog, setting your training efforts back.

Your Voice Is a Natural Tool

Unless you have lost your voice due to injury or illness, this important training tool is with you at all times. Because people tend to be verbal—making words or sounds in response to what goes on around us—using your voice as a training tool is easy.

Your timing in producing a verbal response to your dog's actions is very fast. It's important to acknowledge your dog when she does something right—at the moment she does it. You can say "Yes!" instantly to mark that action, making it easier for your dog to understand what you want.

Timing is also important if you decide to use your voice to interrupt behaviors that you don't want to repeat. A harsh "Ack!" is usually all that's necessary. Just like the "yes" to mark good behavior, the interruption should be said as the dog is making the mistake.

Dogs Are Verbal

The concept of verbal cues is not foreign to dogs. If you have watched a mother dog teaching her puppies, you know that she can be quite verbal. She'll murmur to her puppies as she's cleaning them and she will use a high pitched bark to invite them to play. She will use a soft play growl when playing tug of war with one of the puppies.

Some people who are not familiar with canine communication are startled when they hear a mother dog let one of her puppies know when the puppy has made a mistake. When Claire, a black tri-colored Australian shepherd, had her litter of eight puppies, she was a patient mother and spent a lot of time with her babies. She cared for them, played with them, and helped them explore their limited world. However, if one of the puppies was out of line—such as biting her ear with sharp puppy teeth—she would growl. That growl sounded like she was going to eat the puppy alive—a deep rumbling thunder. But the puppy understood and would stop biting her ear.

Tone Is Important

You wouldn't be able to exactly mimic a mother dog, and there is no reason for you to have to. Dogs learn easily and are adaptable.

Communication is easier, however, if you use a higher-pitched tone of voice for marking the right actions and for praising your dog for a good job. This higher-pitched tone doesn't have to be really high—no need to be squeaky—but just a little higher pitched than your normal speaking voice. Copy the kids in your neighborhood when they see the ice cream truck coming down the street.

If you need to use your voice to interrupt bad behaviors, use a tone that is deeper than your normal speaking voice. That "ack" sound mentioned earlier works fine and is easy to say with a deep voice.

When you ask your dog to do something, use your normal speaking voice. Baby talk is unnecessary; just talk to your dog as you would anyone else.

No Need to Yell

There is no need to yell or scream at your dog when training her. Dogs can hear very well, and yelling and screaming can be intimidating—even frightening—to your dog.

If your dog is ignoring you, then you need to work on your dog training techniques to teach her to pay attention. Yelling is not going to make her pay more attention.

If your dog knows you're upset with her, sniffing the ground is a stress reliever. She's telling you that she's not a threat and asking you to calm yourself. That sniffing may not be a lack of attention so much as your dog trying to change your behavior.

Finding the Right Motivators

Motivators are exactly that: items that will help motivate your dog to cooperate with your training efforts. Although many dog breeds were bred to work for people, they are still more interested in pleasing themselves than pleasing you most of the time. Things that make your dog happy can help motivate her to work with you.

Ideally, with practice, the training itself and your positive reactions to your dog's efforts will become motivators for your dog. But this isn't going to happen right away.

Choose Good Foods

Food treats are great motivators for most dogs. If your dog likes just about anything that bears a resemblance to something edible, super! That will make your training much easier. If your dog likes certain foods but is picky, then you're going to have to work a little harder to find two or three things that your dog will eat.

When choosing the treats, choose good foods rather than commercial junk food treats. Don't use treats loaded with artificial preservatives, colorings, flavoring, or those made primarily of wheat or corn ingredients. These aren't good for your dog.

You're going to be using a lot of treats so it's much better to choose foods that have a good smell, taste good to your dog, and are healthy. Cooked beef, turkey, chicken, and other meats that are not greasy are good treats. Avoid gravy and spices. Cheeses are good. Many dogs love bits of carrots and apples.

If your dog has a problem with her weight, cut back on her daily food a little bit to make up for the additional treats. Just keep an eye on her weight so you can make changes as needed.

Toys and Balls

If your dog is not a food hound, you'll need to find some other things to motivate her. Dogs who love to retrieve and have a favorite ball or flying disc will be easy to motivate with that toy. Or get a new ball or disc and save it for a training reward.

There is a toy called a foxtail that is a ball with a long silk tail that is similar to a kite's tail. You can use the tail to swing the ball around and toss it; as it flies through the air, the tail flips. Dogs love this toy. The ball is slightly smaller than a tennis ball and the tail is of lightweight fabric, so the whole toy is very compact and easy to carry.

Squeaky toys also make good motivators, especially for dogs who like to chase small animals. You might want to find a couple small toys that are easy to carry with your training gear. Try to find one or two toys with different-sounding squeakers, too.

Tug Toys

For a number of years, trainers urged dog owners not to play tug of war with their dogs. It wasn't that tug of war was wrong, but rather that it needed to be done right. Tug games are fine as long as the dog will give up and stop tugging when you ask her to. If the dog gets over stimulated by the game, you need to be able to control the game, stop her, and have her calm down.

Tug of war, however, can be a great motivator. This is especially true if the only time she gets to play the tug game is during training sessions.

There are many commercially available tug toys and any one of these will be fine. Choose one that fits your dog's mouth—neither so small that your big dog could choke on it nor so large that your small dog can't grab it. The tug should be sturdy, too, especially if you have a medium or large dog with strong jaws and teeth.

Choosing a Collar

You can't train your dog until you can communicate with her. While you and your dog work on perfecting your communication skills, your training tools—especially a leash attached to a collar—can help you both control your dog and keep her safe. Plus, the collar can be a part of your communication.

No one collar is right for every dog. You may need to try more than one to find the right collar for your dog; just keep in mind any collar should be kind, humane, and an aid to your training program.

Which Tool Will Work Best?

Buckle Collar

This collar, which closes with a buckle or quick release closure, allows you to restrain your dog with a leash attached. It's fine for a dog who doesn't fight the leash. If your dog pulls hard, this isn't the right collar.

Martingale Collar

This collar consists of two loops; one goes around the dog's neck while the smaller loop goes through both ends of the larger loop and attaches to the leash. When the dog pulls, this will tighten and allow you to communicate with the dog.

Head Halters

The head halter works much like a halter on a horse. The dog is gently guided by the leash that is attached to the halter under the dog's chin. The dog should not be allowed to lunge because doing so could wrench her neck.

Use Only with Professional Help

Several tools should be used only with a dog training professional's recommendation and supervision, if at all. This is because some commonly available tools can be harmful to your dog when used incorrectly or for the wrong purpose.

Slip Collar

A slip collar—chain or fabric—constricts when pulled tight by either the dog or the leash. When used correctly, this can be an effective training tool. When used incorrectly, it can choke the dog; therefore, it should never be tight on the dog's neck.

Prong Collar

Prong collars do not constrict on the dog's neck and so do not choke her. However, the inward facing prongs can hurt; especially when used with force. These can be used effectively on some dogs but are too much correction for many dogs.

Electronic Collar

Electronic collars provide electrical stimulation, usually via a remote triggered by the trainer. These are often used by field and gun dog trainers but require specific knowledge and excellent timing. When used incorrectly or on the wrong dog they can be harmful.

Harnesses

There are a number of different types of harnesses commercially available. Most are designed for specific uses, including pulling a wagon or sled, tracking, to keep safe in a car, or to walk without pulling. Most harnesses are not multi-purpose so it is important to use the correct harness for your goal.

Dog training shouldn't be harmful to your dog. Use tools that you can use safely that will aid in your communication efforts and won't harm your dog.

Pulling Harness

This is not a harness for walking your dog. These harnesses make it easier for a dog to pull a wagon. This harness keeps her front legs free of restraint so she can reach forward easily. The harnesses are well padded.

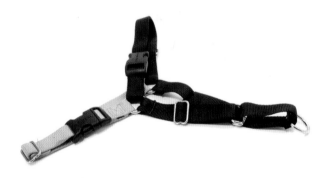

Seat Belt Harness

This harness is not for walking but instead is designed to keep your dog restrained and safe in your car. Each maker has individual designs but there is always a way to hook the harness to the seat belt itself or the seat belt mechanism.

Sport Harnesses

Some sports use a specific harness. The tracking harness, for example, is designed so the dog can lower her head to the ground so she can follow a track. Other harnesses for sports have designs to enable the dog to do what is needed.

No Pull Harness

These harnesses are designed to prevent the dog from pulling while walking. There are a variety of designs; some make it uncomfortable for the dog to pull while others cause the dog to turn away from the path of travel. Use with caution and watch for soreness.

Choosing a Leash

Think of the leash as an umbilical cord between you and your dog. With the leash, you can keep your dog safe by preventing her from dashing away from you. The leash keeps your dog close to you so you can teach her and it helps you communicate with your dog as you begin the training process. When you have the leash on your dog you can also prevent some problem behaviors from occurring.

The length of the leash is important. A 4- to 6-foot leash is the easiest to use during training. If you have a medium- to large-size dog, a shorter leash—often called a traffic leash—is nice when walking your dog, but it's too short for training sessions. A longer leash—10 to 20 feet—is great when you're teaching the Come but it's way too much leash to keep controlled during other exercises.

The clip on the leash needs to be strong and sturdy. An inexpensive clip is a cheap clip, and those often break. However, if you have a toy or small breed dog, don't use a huge clip that would hold a German Shepherd. That will be much too heavy for your tiny dog's neck.

Appropriate Leashes

Web or Woven
Nylon and cotton web or woven leashes are soft on your hands and can be easily washed. These leashes are lightweight and come in narrow widths which can be used for toy breed dogs. Wider leashes are strong enough for large dogs.

Leather
Leather leashes have been traditionally used by long-time dog trainers. The longer a leather leash has been used, the softer and more pliable the leash gets. Available in many widths and styles, leather leashes can be braided, stitched, or may be a combination of both.

Climbing Rope Leashes
The ropes are round, with cloth covering an inner core. One company is actually making leashes out of previously used climbing ropes. The leashes come in several different weights and widths, and a large variety of colors. The leads are soft on the hands and easy to hold.

Avoid These

Chain Leash
These are hard on the owner's hands and can cause injuries to the dog's mouth or teeth.

Bells and Whistles
No whistle, beep, or other gadget will help your dog walk better—training will.

Elastic Leash
These are designed not to put pressure on the dog when she pulls—but you'll be teaching her not to pull in the first place.

Retractable Leashes
These "reward" pulling by giving your dog more leash that she can potentially wrap around trees or legs. The makers' websites list pages of warnings.

Chapter 7

Tips for Training Success

- Develop a vocabulary
- Pay attention to your timing
- Your dog earns his freedom
- What to do when he gets into trouble

Training your dog doesn't have to be difficult. This chapter offers a number of training tips that will make the process easier for you and your dog. Some of these tips will require a little planning, or perhaps a change in your household routine. But most will be easy to implement; the hardest part will simply be remembering to use the tips.

One of the easiest ways to increase your training success is by learning how to use your voice. Varying your tone of voice helps gain your dog's attention when you speak to him. But a vocabulary will help, too. He already reacts to some specific words that mean good things to him such as "ball," "walk," "dinner," "cookie," and "ride," so teaching him some specific words for training will help tremendously.

Another important training tip is to acknowledge your dog's behavior instantly. Praise or interruptions given too early or too late simply are not effective. Learning to use timing correctly takes practice, but it's worth the effort because it helps both communication and learning.

A number of training and behavior problems can be prevented by restricting your dog's freedom, both in the house and outside. A dog who doesn't yet understand the rules of his world will get into trouble. His world should have narrow boundaries until he's ready for more freedom.

When your dog does get into the trash cans, chews up a shoe, or dashes out an open door, what should you do? What shouldn't you do? Mistakes and accidents are going to happen and how you handle them will be important.

Training tips are exactly that: tidbits of information to help make the training easier for both you and your dog. These tips will also help you succeed at setting your goals and following through with them. Plus, these tips aren't etched in stone; you may find that certain things work better for your dog than others.

Build a Vocabulary

You understand the importance of your tone of voice. Using a higher-pitched tone for praise and a deeper tone to interrupt bad behavior mimics canine verbalizations. With varied tones your dog doesn't have to stop and think about (or translate) what you're trying to say. This is going to be important throughout your training, but it's vital as you first begin the training process.

Build a vocabulary. Your dog probably already knows certain words; the names of his favorite toys, the words you say when it's meal time, as well as "walk" and "car." But he can learn a quite extensive vocabulary, and now is the time to begin teaching it.

Everyone who spends time with the dog needs to use the same words in the same situations. For example, to ask your dog to wait in the car and not jump out until you have the leash on him you might say, "Buster, wait." If someone else says, "Don't jump," your dog will not understand. Consistency is important.

Words must have only one meaning. For example, people tend to use the word "down" for many things. If your dog jumps up and you and you say, "Buster, down," what is he going to think when you tell him to get down off the furniture and to lie down on the floor? Come up with some specific vocabulary words and be consistent.

Marker and Praise

You will need a word that you can say quickly in a happy tone of voice to mark actions you like. Many people like, "Yes!" because that will come naturally to you. It's important to have a marker so you can let the dog know without hesitation and without any doubt on his part exactly what you like.

You should also have some words you can use as praise. They can be, "Good boy!" or "Thank you!" These should also be said in a happy tone of voice.

For example, as your dog sits, at the instant his hips touch the ground you can say, "Yes!" Then you can follow up with, "Good boy, Buster." The yes will mark the action you like and the good boy words are rewards.

Just as treats can be a lure and then a reward, so can your voice. The difference with your words is primarily the timing, but with use your dog will also learn that "yes" said at specific times has a special meaning.

Interruption

An interruption is exactly that; you interrupt an action you don't want your dog to do. Many owners will use miscellaneous sounds as interruptions. For example, if you have a book in your hand when you see your dog stick his head in the kitchen trash can, you can drop the book on the table. The sound doesn't have to be loud or violent; it just needs to get the dog's attention.

A verbal interruption works under the same principle. Usually the word "no" isn't recommended as that is used so much in daily conversations. Following along with that thought, using a sound such as "Ack!" often works well. It's a nonsense sound, but when used with a firm tone of voice the dog learns that it means "Stop what you're doing."

Names of Exercises

As you begin teaching your dog, each exercise will have a name. You can use that name to teach your dog, or make up your own. You may be more comfortable in another language or you might prefer to use different words than everyone else uses.

Your dog won't care what words you use, so choose anything you like. What is important is that once you start teaching a particular word, don't change it. Although your dog can learn the new word, it will initially be confusing.

Be Interesting

When you talk to your dog and train him, be interesting to him. Make eye contact, smile, and use your voice in interesting ways. Make funny noises and have fun.

There are a lot of things that will be distracting to your dog as you're trying to train him. Your dog thinks other dogs are worth paying attention to, as are cats, wild rabbits, balloons, kites, seagulls, children, and so much more. The world is an interesting place.

You don't have to be silly if that's embarrassing for you. But you can still work on being interesting enough that your dog pays more attention to you. Play around a little and watch your dog's reactions.

Limit Your Dog's Freedom

Dogs have no idea that the world they live in can be dangerous. Dashing out the front door or the gate can cause them to become lost or hit by a car.

Your home has dangers to your dog, too. If his access isn't restricted until he's mentally grown up and well trained, he could easily hurt himself, become sick, or worse. Freedom may be a wonderful ideal but it isn't necessarily safe—especially for dogs.

Restrictions in the House

Restricting your dog's freedom in the house is necessary until he's mentally mature and well trained. Mental maturity can be reached at anywhere from 18 months of age for some small dogs to 3 or 4 years of age for some large and giant breeds. When your dog can be said to be well trained depends on your training efforts and skills. Most dogs should have their freedom in the house restricted until at least until 2 years of age.

This can be accomplished in several different ways:

- **Crate:** A crate makes a great bed for dogs, and your dog should spend his nights in the crate. He can also spend some time in it now and then throughout the day, but he should not spend all day, every day in the crate. That is not good for him.

- **Exercise pen:** This is a foldable, portable fence that can be used to keep your dog contained to a small area. It's great to set up so your dog can be in a room with you, but at the same time it keeps your dog restricted to a certain space.

- **Baby gates:** A baby gate across a doorway or two, or across a hall, can also restrict your dog's access to parts of the house.

- **Leash:** With your dog on leash and the leash tucked into your pocket or waistband, you can keep your dog close and supervised.

The goal of restricting your dog's freedom in the house is to protect him from danger and to prevent him from getting into trouble. At the same time, you can teach him what he can do, where he can play, and what he can play with. As he matures and these new rules are well understood, then he can have more freedom in the house.

Limited Freedom Outside

Although there are just as many dangers in the house as outside, the ones outside are often more tempting to your dog. A squirrel may cause your dog to try and escape from your yard. A bicyclist going down the street might incite your dog's chase instincts, and again he'll try and escape.

There are dangers inside a securely fenced yard. One of the first training tips for keeping your dog safe in the yard is to dog-proof it thoroughly and put away anything that can be chewed or otherwise damaged by your dog.

Your fence must also be secure. Your dog shouldn't be able to dig under it, climb or jump over it, or go through it. If you can't do this, then consider a dog run. You might prefer to give your dog the entire back yard to play in, but if you can't make the yard safe and secure, then a dog run is a better idea. He can have run of the yard when you supervise him, so you can teach him.

Keeping your dog safe outside also means keeping a leash on him. Not only do most states and localities now have leash laws, but a leash can prevent your dog from getting into trouble. He should be off leash only in a securely fenced area; nowhere else.

When to Allow More Freedom

There is no timetable for when to allow your dog more freedom. Before you give him more freedom, take a look at his behavior. If he's compliant with your wishes, follows your directions, and is not getting into trouble, then begin giving a little more leeway.

Perhaps take down one baby gate or keep one bedroom door open. Watch him for several days and see how he does. If he's doing well, then give him a little more freedom.

When Your Dog Makes a Mistake

If your dog does something you consider wrong, keep in mind that it isn't necessarily a problem to him. Your dog has no idea why chewing a chew bone made out of leather is okay but chewing your leather shoes is wrong. Nor does he know why finding food in the kitchen trash can is a problem.

It's important to look at each mistake as a training opportunity. This is one more thing you need to teach your dog—until you teach him, he doesn't know not to do it.

Catch Him In the Act

If you catch your dog in the act of making a mistake—perhaps with his head in the kitchen trash can—you can interrupt him. As has been discussed previously, an interruption is something that distracts your dog from the unwanted behavior.

The best training tip for this situation is that this is not the time to scream and holler. Do not grab your dog and shake the stuffing out of him. Fear is not a good teacher.

Then, if you need to for your sake, remove your dog from the scene. If he made a mess, chewed up your good shoes, or destroyed something expensive, getting your dog out of the way is usually a good idea so you don't do something you might regret.

You See the Mess Later

If you aren't able to catch your dog in the act of doing something wrong and he's nowhere to be seen, don't do anything to him. Screaming, hollering, shaking him by the collar, or dragging him to the mess is not going to stop it from happening in the future.

He may be worried about you in the future; especially when you walk into the situation again. But he's not going to associate that punishment with something he did hours ago. Dogs live in the moment.

Remove your dog from the scene, calmly, and then clean up the mess. Keep in mind he did this because it appealed to him in some manner, but he didn't do it to you personally.

How You Should Handle It

Once your dog is out of the way, the mess is cleaned up, and you've had a chance to take a deep breath and relax, then you can think about the situation. You don't want to react in anger, even if the dog has caused some damage that will be expensive to repair or replace.

Rather than look upon incidents such as this as something the dog did wrong, think about it as your mistake. Perhaps you gave him too much freedom, or you haven't dog-proofed that area and left things within reach. Maybe he hasn't yet been taught to ignore these items.

As you calmly think about what happened, create a plan so it won't happen again. Think about prevention and training.

Part 3

The Basic Exercises

Living with a dog who makes frequent mistakes is incredibly difficult, so housetraining is considered the first of the basic training exercises.

Sit, Down, and Stay help teach your dog that he can hold still when asked to do so. The Release communicates to your dog when he's free to move around. Teaching the Come means your dog will come to you immediately without any detours. Watch Me and Leave It add to your dog's useful skills, while Let's Go and Heel will make walking your dog a joy rather than a chore.

Chapter 8

Housetraining

Housetraining a dog is the process of teaching the dog to relieve herself in a specific spot, or to try to relieve herself when you ask. Housetraining also means that the dog will not relieve herself inside any building unless she's been taught to go on pads or in a doggy litter box. Last but certainly not least, housetraining also includes teaching the dog how to let you know she needs to go.

Housetraining is easy when you take into account your dog's natural instincts to keep her bed and living area clean. Keep to a schedule so your dog gets outside on time, use your training skills to teach her, and have patience. Most dogs will learn housetraining skills quite easily.

Some variations might be needed depending on your dog's situation and past experiences. A newly adopted dog, for example, will need time to get used to her new home, yard, and routine. A male who has a habit of marking (lifting his leg to urinate) vertical surfaces will need to be treated differently than a puppy. But don't worry; these and other situations will be discussed.

Using a crate is recommended for most dogs. Not only does the crate utilize your dog's instinct to keep her bed clean, it also prevents her from getting into trouble in other ways. Plus, because she has to hold her urine and bowels for gradually increased periods of time, the crate helps build bowel and bladder control.

A Goal for All Dogs

Housetraining requires you to establish a schedule for making sure your dog gets outside. The more you can stick to that schedule, the easier this process will be for your dog. You will also need to teach your dog where you want her to relieve herself, teach her a word that means she should try to go, and then praise her for going. In other words, you're very much a part of this; you cannot just send her outside and expect her to become well housetrained.

Teaching a Puppy

Most puppies have a strong instinct to keep their bed clean. They will start toddling away from their mother and littermates to relieve themselves when they are just a few weeks old, as soon as they can get their legs working right.

You can use this instinct to help your housetraining efforts by using a crate. It is important however to never leave the puppy in the crate so long that she must relieve herself there. Once she has relieved herself in her crate a few times, she will lose the need to keep her bed clean.

Puppies between 8 and 12 weeks of age will need to go outside at least once during the night. By 12 to 14 weeks of age, the puppy should be able to sleep through the night.

During the day, young puppies need to go outside immediately after waking up, after eating, after playing, and about once every hour to hour and a half. Gradually—very gradually—she will be able to go longer between trips outside. By 5 months of age, she will be able to go for 3 hours between trips outside.

That said, every puppy is an individual and will learn and develop bowel and bladder control at her own rate. There are often variances, even among littermates.

The Newly Adopted Dog

The newly adopted adult dog will need to figure out where she is and get to know her new people. She may be worried, excited, or a combination of both.

While she's learning all about her new home, begin the housetraining process as if she's never been housetrained. This will give you a chance to show her where to go and to teach her a vocabulary.

If she was housetrained in her previous home, the process will go quickly. But if she had some housetraining problems in her first home and you've seen some accidents since you brought her home, going through the housetraining process will help you teach her.

A Dog with Bad Habits

If you have a dog with poor housetraining skills or a dog who lifts his leg to urinate on vertical surfaces, you will need to start the housetraining at the beginning, as if the dog is a puppy, and re-teach all the skills. Don't assume your dog knows anything.

As you begin all over again, have your carpets professionally cleaned all the way through to the pads. Use a black light (at night with all other lights turned off) to check for urine spots; urine glows under black light. Clean every single spot with a cleaner made specifically for pet urine. Be thorough about the cleaning. If any smells remain in the house, changing her habits will be more difficult.

For the leg lifter, check with the black light to find everything he has urinated on and clean those items. Don't forget to clean under them, too, as urine can run down and puddle under the table leg or other items. Check the back of the sofa and other furniture and floor-length drapes, too.

Crate Training

A crate can provide your dog with a bed and a place of security, as well as serve as a house-training tool. All dogs, wild and domesticated, are den animals. They prefer a safe place to sleep. That's why dogs often curl up to nap under the foot of the recliner or under a table.

You can use this instinct to find a safe place and combine it with the dog's need to relieve herself away from her bed as a part of her house-training. The crate can also help prevent other bad behaviors—such as destroying the house when you're not home—during puppyhood and adolescence.

The Crate Is Not a Jail

It's important to remember that a crate is not a jail. Yes, it does confine the dog but when introduced correctly most dogs walk in without dislike or hesitation and look upon it as their place of quiet and security. If the crate door is left open, many dogs will go to the crate on their own to get away from household disruptions or to take a nap.

Plus, the dog will not have to be confined for her lifetime. The crate will be used with the door shut for puppyhood and adolescence, or while changing a bad habit. Then the door can be left open or even removed and the dog can continue to use the crate as a bed.

If you like to travel and want to bring your dog with you, a crate is important. Many hotels will not charge an extra pet fee if the dog is crated.

Types of Crates

Plastic Crate

These generally come in two sections and join together with screws or fasteners. The solid bottom will protect the flooring underneath. Dogs tend to be comfortable in these crates, which are den-like and secure. The downside to these crates is they are bulky, even in pieces. Airlines require these crates to transport a dog.

Wire Crate

These often have a door on the front and on one side so the crate has more placement options. A removable plastic pan is usually on the bottom of the crate. It is open to the breezes, which is better in hot weather. Because it is so open, many dogs feel vulnerable in this crate rather than secure—try covering part of the crate with a towel or blanket.

Soft-Sided Crate

These are collapsible, portable crates made of nylon or other strong materials. People who travel to dog shows or other events often use these crates. These should not be used as a dog's first crate because dogs can chew or rip the material to escape.

Introducing the Crate

Toss in Treats

You want your dog to associate going in the crate with good things; so to begin introducing it, you'll toss treats inside. Have the crate door open and have a handful of good treats your dog really likes. Let your dog sniff the treats and toss one just inside the crate. Praise your dog when she gets it. Gradually begin throwing the treats farther inside.

Feed Dog in Crate

When your dog is going in and out of the crate for treats with no hesitation, then begin feeding her in the crate. With the door open, place your dog's food just inside the crate so she can stand outside and just reach in with her head. Each subsequent meal, move the bowl more toward the back of the crate, but leave the door open.

3

Close the Door

When your dog is going inside the crate to eat with no problems, then for her next meal feed her in the crate and close the door. Let her out after she's eaten unless she's barking or pawing at the door. If she is, just wait until she calms herself and then let her out.

4

Make It the Bed

You can now begin using the crate as your dog's bed. Continue to offer a treat as you put your dog to bed. At the same time, teach him the word you wish to use. Some owners say "kennel" while others prefer "go to bed." No matter what you use, be consistent and praise your dog when she goes into the crate.

The Housetraining Process

The easiest way to housetrain your dog is to keep the training simple. Not only is this easier for you and your dog, but it also makes it easier to gain cooperation from everyone else involved with the dog. If things are too complicated, many people won't work with you.

Use the Schedule

Your dog needs to go outside after waking up, after play times, after eating, and every few hours in between. Puppies will need to go out even more often.

Plus, your dog needs to be fed at regular times each day. Play times, grooming, training, and walks should also be a part of her day.

Create a schedule and post it in a prominent place so everyone in the household understands it. If one person expects someone else to take the dog out and no one does, the dog isn't at fault for an accident.

The Magic Word

Choose a word or two that will tell your dog to try to relieve herself. Many people use a phrase such as "Go potty," but some family members might be embarrassed to say that in public. You might say, "Get busy." Choose a word or phrase that will work for everyone in the family. After all, your dog doesn't care what words you use.

In the beginning, softly say, "Get busy," as your dog is relieving herself so you can connect the word and the action. Say it softly so you don't interrupt her.

After a couple of weeks, say the words as you walk her to the spot where you want her to relive herself. In other words, tell her what you want her to do now.

Where to Go

Choose where you wish your dog to relieve herself throughout the day. Ideally your dog should have easy access to this spot, as well as some peace and quiet. If the spot is busy it will be too easy for her to get distracted.

It should be easy for you to clean, too. After all, this is going to be an ongoing chore. If it's a hard spot to clean, it won't work.

Every once in a while, take her out of your yard to other places and ask her to relieve herself in those spots, also. She needs this in case you travel, go visiting, or are otherwise away from her yard.

Walk your dog on a leash to her spot in the yard. Without a leash, she may come with you or not; she might try to play instead of relieve herself. On leash, you can walk her to her spot, tell her "Get busy," and keep her there until she relives herself.

As she's finishing her business, softly praise her, "Good to get busy!" When she's done, praise her more enthusiastically, "Good girl! Yeah!" Let her know this is exactly what you wanted her to do, where you wanted her to do it.

Limit Her Freedom

Continue to limit your dog's freedom. If you don't and she sneaks off to relieve herself in various places in the house, she will have taught herself that going potty in the house is fine.

Don't let that happen. Use the crate, exercise pen, and baby gates. You can also leash her and keep her with you. Close doors to other rooms. It really doesn't matter how you limit her, just do it in the easiest manner for you, your family, and your home.

Litter Box and Potty Pads

Sometimes taking the dog outside to relieve herself is not possible. If you work long hours each day and can't get home in the middle of the day, providing your dog with a place inside to relieve herself is a great idea. People who have disabilities that prevent them from taking the dog outside may also appreciate this, as do people who live in a severe climate that could be potentially dangerous for their dog.

Potty Pads

These pads of absorbent material have a liner that prevents moisture from going through, much like bed liners or diapers. Originally marketed as housetraining aids for puppies, they serve the same purpose as doggy litter boxes.

Sometimes the potty pads are simply placed on the floor, especially a flooring such as tile that won't be harmed if the dog misses the pad. Other dog owners will place the pad in a litter box where the walls of the box provide a boundary. This provides more guidance for the dog—some dogs will get their paws on the pads yet relieve themselves off the pads.

Litter Boxes

Most people associate litter boxes with indoor cats, but in the past few years many small dogs have been introduced to litter boxes, too. A litter box is usually a plastic pan such as a large cat litter box or a mortar pan from a home supply or hardware store. The litter should be made specifically for dogs out of pine, wheat, or other natural products. Do not use clumping cat litter, as it can be dangerous for dogs if they lick it off their paws.

Some dog owners get a square of grass sod each weekend and place it in the litter box. Many dogs prefer to use grass, so this makes it easy to teach the dog to use the litter box. Replacing the grass each weekend prevents the bad smell that would occur if the dog used the same square of grass (and soil) for a longer period of time.

Squares of artificial turf can also be used. Cut to the size of the litter box, the turf can be pulled up regularly, washed and dried, and the box can be washed. Several pieces of artificial turf would allow for a couple to be washed and dried while another one is being used.

Training

Teaching your dog to use either of these tools is just like training your dog to go outside. To start, put your dog on leash and take her to the box or pad at a time when you know she has to go. Let her sniff the litter or pad without giving her any cues.

Stay there even if she gets antsy or acts confused. When she does relieve herself, softly repeat the words, "Get busy." When she's done, praise her enthusiastically. When she knows the words, start asking her to relieve herself.

As with all housetraining, limit her freedom in the house. Leave her in an exercise pen with her box or pads when you're gone or unable to supervise her.

The most common problem with this training is that most owners stop giving the dog positive reinforcement far too soon. When the dog is beginning to go to the box or pads, the owner thinks the dog is trained and they take that for granted. The dog, who is no longer being praised, stops going to the box or pads.

Housetraining Problems

Most dogs become reliably housetrained easily; many with little help from their owners. However, at times, confusion sets in or communication breaks down and housetraining problems ensue.

Puppy Confusion

Puppies require your help. Go outside with your puppy, teach her the verbal cue, wait for her to go, and then praise her. She'll learn.

However, you also need to be patient. Every puppy will learn these skills at her own rate. Don't compare your puppy to your neighbor's or friend's puppies. Help your puppy learn at her own rate and help her succeed.

The most common problem arises when owners send the puppy outside on her own. The owner is no longer providing positive reinforcement for the puppy relieving herself outside. Perhaps even more important, when the puppy comes back in, the owner has no idea if the puppy has relieved herself or not.

Adult Goes on Carpet

The first thing you need to do is restrict the dog's freedom to a crate, exercise pen, and on a leash with you. She is not allowed free run of the house where she can sneak away to relieve herself.

Then you need a black light (from the local hardware store). At night—with all other lights turned off—find all the urine spots glowing under the black light. Shampoo your carpet with a shampoo made specifically for pet urine. After you have cleaned the carpet (and the rest of the house) check again with the black light to make sure you've got it all.

Then begin taking your dog outside on leash as you would do with a puppy. You are re-teaching housetraining skills from the beginning. The only difference is that your adult dog has a bad habit established, and that will take longer to change than it will take to teach most puppies.

The Leg Lifter

Leg lifters are unpredictable problems. Some will be very good and mark nothing in the house until a guest arrives. Then they will urinate on the guest's purse or luggage.

Use a black light to find all the urine and clean it up. Don't leave anything for your dog to smell.

Then go to a pet store or online pet supply catalog and—if your marker is a male—find some belly bands that will fit him. These are straps the go around the dog's belly that hold a pad against his penis. If he tries to mark, he urinates in the pad. If your marker is a female, get the pants made for female dogs in season; these will work the same way.

Severely curtail freedom as you re-train your problem dog; keep your dog in a crate or an exercise pen, or on a leash with you.

A Change in Habits

If your dog has been reliably housetrained and suddenly begins making mistakes, talk first to your veterinarian. Tell your veterinarian there has been a change in housetraining and specify whether it has been urination of defecation.

Many medical issues or medications can cause your dog to need to urinate more frequently. Urinary tract infections and diabetes are common causes, as are steroid medications. You and your veterinarian can discuss her health, what's going on, and decide on a plan.

Gastrointestinal upsets tend to cause diarrhea or a change in defecation. A change in food, different treats, or too many snacks can lead to a change, also. Garbage-itis—the informal name for when dogs raid the kitchen trash and eat something they shouldn't—will cause gastrointestinal upsets. Again, talk to your veterinarian about what's going on.

Chapter 9

Teaching Sit, Sit Stay, and Release

These first three exercises—Sit, Sit Stay, and Release—are the foundation for everything you teach your dog in the future. No matter what you do—teach household rules, social manners, participate in canine sports, or compete—these first three exercises will be needed.

In addition, Sit and Sit Stay can prevent a number of problem behaviors. By learning to sit and stay at an open door, your dog won't be dashing outside. When your dog can sit nicely for petting, he isn't jumping on people. Sit and Sit Stay are wonderful first foundation exercises.

As you teach these first three exercises, you will also get a chance to practice your training skills. The chapters in Part 1 provided all of the background information for you; now you'll get a chance to implement it.

As you get started, keep in mind your dog has no idea why you're doing this. Don't get impatient when he doesn't understand and don't get angry if he's distracted or doesn't cooperate. Instead, try harder to gain his interest with your voice, petting, and food treats.

Plus, for your first several training sessions, choose a nice quiet place with few distractions and have some really good treats in your pocket. Make sure your dog is on leash, take a deep breath, smile, and have some fun with your dog.

Every exercise you do with your dog will begin with his name. This is the easiest way to let him know you're talking to him and desire his attention. "Sweetie, sit," for example.

Teaching Sit

When your dog sits, his shoulders will remain up with his front legs braced, while his hips are on the ground. When you ask him to sit, he will remain in this position until you release him. You don't want him to lie down or get up and walk away; he is to remain in this position.

The words you will use are, "Sweetie, sit." When you are ready for him to move, you will release him. (See the Release exercise at the end of this chapter.) In between, you will praise him for his cooperation.

Two techniques are used for teaching the Sit. The first is a lure and reward technique that uses a food treat to help your dog assume the position you want. The food also becomes the reward once your dog is sitting. The second technique, just in case your dog decides to ignore you and the treat, will use your hands to help your dog sit.

Using the Lure

Treat at Nose

Have your dog on leash and hold the leash in one hand. Your dog can be standing by your side or in front of you, as long as he's within reach. Have a treat in your right hand and then let him sniff it. You can even let him lick it to get even more interested.

Treat Up and Back

As your dog sniffs the treat, slowly move it up and back over the dog's head. Hold the treat close to your dog's nose so that as you move the treat, his nose will follow it. As his head and nose go up and back, it will be more comfortable for him to sit. As he begins to sit, tell him, "Sweetie, sit!"

Give the Treat

As soon as your dog's hips touch the ground, praise him, "Sweetie, good sit! Yeah!" Pop the treat in his mouth and pet him. He's to hold the sit position until you release him, so if he's prone to popping right back up, keep a hand on his collar so you can help him remain in the sitting position.

Release

After praising your dog and giving him the treat, you can release him, but only if he's sitting nicely. If he's wiggling, let him calm down—even if it takes a couple of minutes—then you can release him. A Release is a reward so give him a reward for the actions you want repeated.

An Alternate Technique

Hands in Position

Put all your treats in your pocket. With your dog on leash, hold the leash in one hand. Place that hand in front of your dog's collar. Don't hold the collar; just place it there. Your other hand can rest in the middle of your dog's back.

Slide and Tuck

Slide your empty hand down your dog's back past his tail and gently begin to tuck his rear end under him. At the same time, tell him, "Sweetie, sit," and gently push upward with your leash hand. There should be a gentle teeter-totter effect.

In the Sit

As your dog sits, keep the hand holding the leash on the dog's collar if he's wiggly and seems like he's going to pop up. Otherwise, praise and pet him for sitting. Don't give him a treat, however. He gets a treat when he follows the lure in the first technique.

Release

Release him only when he's sitting still. After you have praised and petted your dog, then tell him, "Sweetie, release!" Step back a couple of steps and encourage him to get up. Praise him again.

Do not push down on your dog's hips or in the middle of his back—that will hurt him. It could cause him to fight you. Instead, gently tuck.

Teaching Stay

You will be teaching your dog that when you tell him to stay in a position—first in a Sit and later in a Down—he's to remain in that position until you release him. (See the instruction for Release in the last section of this chapter.) That places a responsibility on you, of course. Never tell him to stay and then walk away and forget him; always go back to him and release him.

As you teach your dog to Sit Stay, remain close to him—within one step away—and at first have him hold still for 5 seconds, then go back to him, praise him, and release him. Over several training sessions, if he's holding still and not making any mistakes, increase the time to 10 seconds, then 15.

Then, gradually increase the distance, taking two steps away from him, and then three. As you teach the Stay, you can increase the time or the distance, but never do both at the same time.

If your dog begins making mistakes, you may be trying to increase the time or distance too quickly. Go back, review the basic steps, and then gradually increase one or the other again to see where the problem is.

Sit Stay

Stay Hand Signal

Have your dog sit and praise him. Hold his leash in your one hand, and tell your dog, "Sweetie, stay," as you give him the stay signal with your other hand. This is an open hand, palm toward your dog's nose, moved up and down as if creating an invisible wall to prevent your dog from moving forward.

One Step Away

Take one step away from your dog while continuing to face him. The leash should remain loose with no tension on the dog's neck. Don't repeat the stay command or talk to him right now. After 5 seconds go back to him, praise him, pet him, and then release him.

Gradually Increase Distance

Over a period of several training sessions and several days, or even a couple of weeks, increase the distance you step away from your dog. Continue to hold the leash just in case your dog decides to move away; you want to be able to stop him and put him back where he started.

Add Distractions

When your dog understands Sit Stay and is doing it well, then it's time to add some distractions. Add distractions at home first—perhaps eat something while your dog is doing a Stay. Then move outside, down the block, and to the nearby park. Just watch your dog and help him succeed.

Introducing Release

You need to a way to show your dog when he's finished a particular exercise and is free to move. This exercise is called the Release and it means he's released from that exercise; he's completed it.

For example, after having your dog sit, you can praise him, and then pat him on the shoulder and tell him, "Sweetie, release!" He will learn that the word "release" and the pat on the shoulder mean he's done; he can get up from the sit, and can move freely for a moment or two.

When you initially say, "Sweetie, release," and pet your dog on the shoulder he won't understand. But if you take a couple steps backward, smile at your dog, and put a little pressure on the leash to encourage your dog to move, he will. Then praise him again.

You will use the Release after most obedience exercises. By doing so you will teach your dog when his attention on you is necessary and when he can relax. When you say his name he should focus on you and when you release him he can look away, sniff, stretch, and be comfortable.

The word "release" is used here, but you can change the vocabulary if you wish. Some dog owners use the word "free;" just chose a word you'll be comfortable using for a while.

Using the Sit Stay

The Sit and Stay are two exercises you will find many uses for once your dog understands them. Not only do these two exercises help teach your dog self-control but they work wonderfully to help keep him safe.

A few ideas for using them include:

- When your dog sits to be petted, he isn't jumping on people. He can sit while you pet and he can sit when guests or neighbors pet him. To help him, just keep a hand on his collar and if he tries to jump up, remind him, "Sweetie, sit. Good!"

- When your dog sits and stays as you're fixing his food he won't be jumping up and knocking the bowls out of your hands. Have another family member help you by having the dog sit and stay as you fix the food. Then after you place the food on the floor, praise your dog and release him.

- Teach him to sit and stay at all open doors to the outside. This can prevent him from dashing out every time a door is opened.

- Have him sit and stay at doors so he doesn't dash inside, too. That way, you can towel him off before coming in when it's raining. Plus, if he waits for permission before coming in, he won't knock people over or barrel into knees.

- Teach him to sit and stay when a gate is opened, too, for the same reasons.

There are many other reasons to teach the Sit and Stay and other applications for it. Have him sit and hold still so you can hook his leash up to his collar before you go for a walk. If he's spinning circles in excitement, it's hard to hook up the leash.

As you teach your dog, take a look at your daily routine. You'll find other ways this and other exercises can be used.

Chapter 10

Teaching Down and Down Stay

Your dog can progress to the exercises in this chapter when she has a good understanding of Sit, Sit Stay, and Release. She doesn't have to master them—that will take practice—but if she is doing them well and is cooperating with you, then you can begin these exercises.

The Down builds on the skills your dog has already learned. If she sits, her hips are already on the floor and all you have to do is lower her front end. Plus, if you ask your dog to sit, you will already have her attention and she's holding still.

The Down exercise will be taught using two different techniques: one technique will use the lure and reward, and the alternative technique will have you shape your dog into the position.

Your dog should learn the Down Stay fairly quickly. She's already been introduced to it as you practiced the Sit Stay, and most dogs are more comfortable when lying down anyway. But as with the Sit Stay, take your time teaching the Down Stay as it does require some self-control on your dog's part.

Teaching Down

When teaching your dog to lie down, you want her to understand that "down" means to lie down on the ground (or floor) until you release her. When she lies down, she should be in a comfortable position with her hips leaned to one side. There's no need for her to be upright on her elbows and hocks. In fact, she's more likely to remain in the position if she's comfortable.

It's important to choose a word for this exercise that has no other meaning for your dog. If you use the word "down" when your dog jumps up on you or gets up on the furniture, using it for this exercise will be confusing. Each word should have only one meaning. When teaching the exercise here, the word "down" will be used; but feel free to use another word when teaching your dog.

Using a Lure

Lure in Front of Nose

Have your dog sit by your side; praise and reward her. Hold the leash in one hand and place that hand on your dog's shoulder. Use no pressure; your hand is to take hold of the collar should your dog wiggle too much. Let her sniff the treat in your other hand.

Bring Her Nose Down

As your dog is sniffing the treat, begin moving it down to her front paws. As her nose follows the treat and she begins to lie down tell her, "Sweetie, down! Good!" Once her nose follows the treat to her paws, then move the treat forward slowly a few inches until her elbows are on the ground.

Praise and Reward

Once your dog's elbows are on the ground, praise her and pop that treat in her mouth. Tell her what a smart, cooperative dog she is. Pet her as she's eating the treat. Keep your leash hand on her shoulders so if she tries to wrestle or pop right back up you can interrupt her.

Release

Your dog shouldn't move from the Down position until you release her. Being praised and getting a treat doesn't mean she can automatically release herself; she needs to wait until you tap her on the shoulder and tell her, "Sweetie, release." If she's anticipating the release, then vary the time before you do it.

Alternative Technique

Reach Over

Have your dog sit by your left side; do not have him sit in front of you as this technique will be ineffective in that position. With the leash held in your right hand, reach toward his right front leg while your left arm goes over your dog's shoulders so you can grasp his left front leg.

Scoop and Down

With one hand on each of your dog's front legs, gently lift them and move them forward slightly as you say, "Sweetie, down." Lower your dog to the floor. If she is prone to popping right back up from the Down, place your left hand on her shoulder so you can calm her with gentle petting.

Body Position

As you lower your dog to the floor, gently turn her front legs toward you (the right) so that her body is in a slight "C" shape. This is more comfortable for most dogs; in this position they are less likely to pop up.

Praise and Release

Praise and pet your dog while she's in the Down position. She is not to pop up on her own; if she does, gently shape her into the Down again. Then release her with the pat on the shoulder and "Sweetie, release."

Teaching Down Stay

Same Hand Signal

Have your dog sit, praise her, and then ask her to lie down, using either Down technique. Praise her in the Down. Tell her, "Sweetie, stay," as you give her the stay signal. This is the same as the hand signal you used for the Sit Stay—open hand, palm toward your dog's nose, moved up and down as if creating an invisible wall to prevent your dog from moving forward.

Remain Close

After telling her to stay, stand up straight but remain next to her. When first learning the Down Stay, sometimes there is confusion and the dog sits because that's where she first learned the Stay. By remaining close, you can place a hand on her shoulder if she tries to get up.

Step Away

When your dog is remaining in the Down without popping up, then begin taking a step or two away. Increase the distance gradually over several training sessions. Then begin increasing the time you ask your dog to stay, from 5 seconds to several minutes.

Pet, Praise, and Release

When your dog has held the Stay, always go back to her to pet and praise her. She should hold the Down Stay while you reward her and then, when you're ready, release her.

As your dog learns the Down Stay and becomes good at it when practicing at home, then gradually increase distractions. If your dog begins making mistakes, you're doing too much too soon.

Using the Down Stay

The primary difference between Sit Stay and Down Stay, other than the obvious position differences, is that your dog can more comfortably hold the Down Stay for a longer period of time. So if you need your dog to hold still for a minute or two, ask her to sit and stay. If you would like her to hold still for longer than a couple of minutes, then have her lie down and stay. As you teach the Down Stay, you'll find that once she understands it, the time she's able to hold still will increase fairly quickly.

Depending on your household routine, you can use the Down Stay in a number of ways:

- Ask her to Down Stay away from the dining room table while the family is eating. This will take practice to teach, but persevere because it prevents the dog from begging.

- Have her Down Stay at your feet in the evening while people are relaxing and watching a favorite show. Release her and play with her during commercials.

- Have her Down Stay when guests come over so she isn't bugging your guests. Put her leash on her before you invite your guests in so you can help her behave.

- Ask her to Down Stay outside the kitchen while you're cooking so you don't trip over her.

- Let her do a Down Stay while the kids are playing so she doesn't jump on or chase the kids.

- She can do a Down Stay while people are playing with the family cat.

Take a look at your normal routine and your daily life with your dog and decide where a little more self-control on her part would be nice. Then help her so she succeeds at this new challenge.

Chapter 11

Teaching Come

- Come is a mandatory skill
- Teach Come with multiple techniques
- Games make training fun

When a dog doesn't come to his owner each and every time he's called, his life is at risk. If he's off leash or his leash breaks, if he dashes out an open gate, or jumps out of the car without permission, without a good response to the Come he could become lost. Many dogs taken in by animal control departments became strays because they didn't return to their owner when called.

Of course, being lost is only one danger he could face. He could also be hit by a car, go hungry, face dangers from people or other animals; the list is long. Plus, you'd be worried and afraid for your dog. Thankfully, you can teach your dog to come to you reliably.

Several techniques are used to teach the Come, and each emphasizes a certain part of the exercise. Teaching your dog with a sound stimulus helps him focus on you when you say, "Sweetie, come!" Teaching him on leash helps him come directly to you without any detours. Teaching him to wait and then come helps him develop more self-control. Each of these techniques will help build a strong reliable Come.

It's important to remember to never scold your dog when you call him. You want to build in your dog a desire to come to you more than anything else in the world. If you scold him, give him a bath after he comes to you, or do anything else he dislikes, then coming to you won't be a priority in his mind. When he comes to you, greet him with open arms, praise him enthusiastically, pop a treat in his mouth, and pet him.

As you're creating this new response to the word "come" and helping building a new habit, don't give your dog a chance to ignore you when you say "come." He's not to be off leash in situations where he can ignore you, nor should you stand in one spot and say "come" over and over again while he ignores you. Instead, be smarter than your dog and think about various situations before you let him run. From now on he must come to you when you call him.

Come with a Sound Stimulus

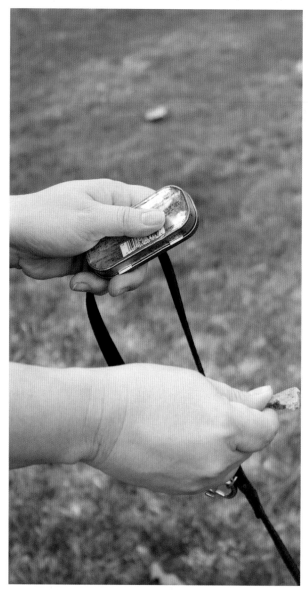

Using a sound stimulus while teaching your dog to come when you call him works because the sound stimulus will gain your dog's attention. So when you call him with your voice he's already focused on you. A sound stimulus often works better than using only your voice because our voices are used so much. Although certain words convey meaning, most of what we say is just noise, and the dog learns to tune us out. A sound stimulus can gain attention so the dog is listening.

Some people use a whistle for this exercise, but the best sound is some hard dog food or treats in a small container. This is a strong reinforcer because your dog already knows this sound; he hears it every day. The sound of the food or treats being rattled in the container, paired with your verbal cue and a treat, is very attractive to your dog.

You won't have to use the shaker for the rest of your dog's life. As with any training tool, the idea of using the shaker is to teach your dog and then continue using it long enough to build a good habit. For most dogs, using the shaker regularly for several months of training will be fine. However, if your dog has some bad habits concerning the Come, you may need to use the shaker for a longer period of time. Keep in mind each dog is unique in temperament, personality, experiences, and habits.

> By having your dog sit when he comes to you, you're teaching him to come to you rather than play keep away or run past you. Plus, when he's sitting, he's not jumping on you for the treat.

Shake and Treat

With your dog on leash and sitting in front of you, hold the leash and shaker in one hand, and a treat in the other. Shake the shaker and pop the treat in your dog's mouth. Don't say anything; this step teaches him that the sound of the shaker means he gets a good treat. Do this 5 or 6 times, take a break, and come back to it. Do this for 2 or 3 days.

Add the Word "Come"

Have your dog on leash, sitting in front of you, with the leash and shaker in one hand and treats in the other. Shake the shaker, say, "Sweetie, come!," praise him, and pop the treat in his mouth. The sound of the shaker and the happy word "come" equal praise and a good treat. Do this 5 or 6 times, take a break, and repeat for 3 days.

Come and Back Away

Now you want to teach your dog that "come" also means move toward you for that praise and treat. With you and your dog in the same positions as before, tell your dog, "Sweetie, come!" as you shake the shaker, and take a few steps backward so your dog follows you. After a few steps, praise him and pop a treat in his mouth.

Come, Back Up, and Sit

Begin in the same position. After calling your dog to come using the shaker and your voice, and taking a few steps backward, stop backing up. When your dog catches up to you, use the treat to signal your dog to sit. When he's sitting, praise him and pop the treat in his mouth.

Come on a Long Leash

Teaching your dog to come on a long leash gives you some additional control. Should your dog dash away or ignore you, with the leash you can restrain him or stop him from running from you. Do not yell or jerk the leash; just prevent him from running from you. Then use the following tips to teach the come.

Dog a Little Farther Away

Your technique for calling your dog when he's a little farther away is the same as in the previous section except your dog doesn't have to be sitting to start. Let him move around, sniff, and be a little distracted. Use your shaker and your voice, praise him, have him sit in front of you, and pop a treat in his mouth.

Reel Him In

If your dog doesn't come to you when you call him, drop the shaker to free your hand. Back away from your dog and use the leash to encourage him to follow you. Praise him as you're reeling in the leash. Have him sit when he catches up to you and then give him the treat. Do not use a harsh tone of voice or pop the leash.

Use Distractions

When your dog learns the Come on a long leash and is responding well, then it's time to add some distractions. Do this gradually by first changing where you train; perhaps from the backyard to the front yard. Then work around some kids at the playground, or other dogs. Use really good treats to lure and reward your dog and use lots of praise.

Teach Wait and Come

You want to teach your dog that "wait" means "Hold this position, but pay attention to me because another command will be following shortly." For example, when you open the car door, you don't want your dog to jump out until you hook up his leash and make sure it's safe for him. So you tell him, "Sweetie, wait," and hook up his leash.

The difference between Stay and Wait is what happens afterward. With both, your dog is to hold still and remain in position when you walk away. With Stay, you always go back to him to praise him and release him. With Wait, you're going to tell him to do something else.

You can tell him it's okay to jump out of the car or jump into the car. You can call him out an open door or gate. You can give him permission to come in the house after toweling off his paws. There are lots of uses for this versatile exercise.

Teaching Wait

Hand Signal and Verbal Cue

Have your dog sit, make the same hand signal you used for Stay, and say, "Sweetie, wait." Take a few steps away from him and stop. After a few seconds, tell your dog, "Sweetie, okay," and holding the leash just walk away. When your dog gets up and follows you, praise him.

Wait at the Gate

With your dog on leash, have him sit inside your yard gate. With the leash in one hand, make the Stay hand signal with the other as you tell your dog, "Sweetie, wait." Open the gate. If your dog dashes, interrupt him verbally, then bring him back and repeat the exercise until he will wait for permission to walk through the gate.

Permission to Come In

Have your dog on leash. Ask him to sit by the door to the house. Tell him to wait and step inside, dropping his leash. Wait a few seconds and open the door, repeating to your dog, "Sweetie, wait." If he holds still, give him permission to come in. If he dashes, grab his leash, put him back in the Sit and repeat the exercise.

Wait for Food Bowl

With the leash on your dog, have him sit, tell him to wait, and drop the leash to the floor. Go fix his dinner and walk back to him. Place his bowl on the floor, and after a few seconds give him permission to move and eat it. If he moves before you give him permission, pick up his leash, take him back to his spot, and repeat the exercise.

Wait and Come

Sit and Hand Signal
Have your dog sit, on leash, and hold the leash in one hand. Praise him for sitting. Use the hand signal for Wait with the other hand and tell him, "Sweetie, wait."

Step Away
After telling your dog to wait, step away from him. How far depends on your dog. If he's doing well on the Stay exercises and you can take three to four steps away, great. If you need to remain closer that's fine, too. Hold the leash as you step away.

Back Away and Come

Let your dog hold still for several seconds after telling him to wait. Then call him, "Sweetie, come," and back away from him for several steps. Dogs like to chase things and when you back away from him, he's more apt to follow you. Plus, this gives him a few more steps to come to you.

Approach You and Sit in Front

Stop backing up, and as your dog catches up to you tell him, "Sweetie, sit." Make the Sit hand signal with a treat in your hand. When he sits, praise him and give him the treat. Remember, having your dig sit in front of you after the Come keeps him focused on you and prevents him from jumping on you or dashing past you.

The Back and Forth Game

The Come is an important exercise—potentially a life-saving one. Although training the Come needs to be taken seriously, your dog doesn't understand that.

Dogs repeat actions that are rewarding to them; you've heard this before. Treats, praise, petting, and fun are important parts of the training for your dog. When he comes to you, cheer him on like the best cheerleader around, "Yeah, good boy! Look at you! Woo hoo!"

Using your voice, see how fast you can get him to run to you. See if you can get him to kick it up into a faster pace and when he does, praise him even more.

Use really good treats that you know he loves. And then pet him. Let him know he's the best, smartest, most awesome dog in the world.

You can also play some games to make the Come fun. By playing a game, you have as much fun as your dog—and while the two of you are having fun, you're still teaching the Come.

What You Need

For this game you'll need a little bit of room and a helper. You can play it back and forth down a hallway, or in the yard. You need a long leash for your dog—20 to 30 feet. You also need some special treats your dog really likes, something he normally doesn't get.

On Your Mark, Get Ready

One person will hold the dog's leash and keep the dog close while the second person walks away. If your leash is twenty feet long, stand that far apart. The person who walks away should try to get the dog excited, "I have cookies! Are you a good boy?"

Sweetie, Come!

When the second person calls the dog, the first person can drop the leash or follow behind holding the leash. It depends on how well your dog is doing with the Come. When the dog reaches the second person, he should sit, then get his praise, petting, and treat.

Repeat with Cheers and Treats

Repeat this by having the dog run back and forth a few times. Make sure the dog is having a great time; this is a game, remember. If you see your dog begin to look bored or slow down—stop the game. Always stop before your dog decides to quit playing.

Chapter 12

Teaching Attention and Leash Skills

Taking your dog for a walk is an integral part of dog ownership. A walk is exercise for both of you, provides opportunities for socialization, and allows the two of you to spend time together. If your dog has poor leash skills, however, a walk isn't fun at all.

Not only that, but your dog can injure herself by lunging at the end of the leash or pulling. She can hurt her trachea, wrench her neck, or damage her shoulders. You can be hurt, too. Hand, arm, and shoulder injuries have resulted from dogs pulling. Even worse injuries can result if your dog lunges and you lose your balance and fall.

Good leash skills begin with teaching your dog to pay attention to you. When she's paying attention you can teach her what you want her to do, including walking nicely on the leash. Watch Me is an attention exercise that will teach her to focus on you, plus you'll learn an attention game that will make the training fun.

There are several ways to teach leash skills. The Heel exercise is a traditional way to teach your dog where to walk with you, and it's an important skill because when your dog is doing this she can do a Watch Me at the same time. While doing a Heel, the two of you are working together as a team. There are a couple of alternative skills that will also teach your dog not to pull.

Teaching Attention

If your dog is easily distracted it can be tough to teach her. After all, your world is full of distractions that range from the family cat at home to butterflies flitting by when you're outside. Depending on your dog's interests, just about anything can be a distraction.

Teaching your dog how to pay attention to you—and rewarding her for her attention—is a great way to make those distractions less appealing to her. The distractions will still be there, but you can make paying attention to you more rewarding for her.

You won't be asking her to focus on you all the time. That's unreasonable. However, when you need her to look at you and ignore the distractions, she'll have the ability to do it.

The Watch Me teaches her to look at you when you ask her to. When she knows this exercise, then you can teach her an attention game based on the Watch Me. It can be challenging at times but that's okay. We want your dog to be able to think and problem solve.

With all of these exercises, practice 5 or 6 times, take a break, and then repeat. These take a lot of concentration and doing them too many times will cause your dog to fail.

Watch Me

Introduce in a Quiet Place

Begin teaching the Watch Me in a quiet location with no distractions. A bathroom or a back hall is good. Have your dog sit, on leash, and hold the leash in one hand. Have a treat in the other hand and let her sniff the treat. Take the treat to your chin as you say, "Sweetie, watch me!" When she looks at you, praise her enthusiastically and pop the treat in her mouth.

One or Two Distractions

When your dog can do the Watch Me in a quiet location, then add one or two minor distractions. Move from the bathroom to the bedroom where the family cat is sleeping on the bed. Or move from the hall to the living room. If your dog gets distracted, interrupt her with a sound and then use the treat to gain her attention again. When she looks at you, praise her and give her the treat.

Go Outside

When your dog is doing the Watch Me well inside with distractions, then move outside. Practice with normal distractions: other dogs, kids, squirrels, and anything else that might cause your dog to look away. And she can look away as long as she looks back at you when you ask her to.

No Jump

If your dog jumps up when you move the treat from her nose to your chin, use your other arm to prevent it. Take hold of her collar and straighten your arm, locking your elbow. Then as you do the Watch Me, if she jumps, your left arm will prevent her from coming up into your face. Tell her, "Ack! No jump!" Then have her sit again.

Attention Game

Game Rules
Sit your dog in front of you, on leash, with leash dropped to the ground, and stand with one foot on the leash. Have some treats in each hand. Let your dog sniff the treats.

Hands Down at Your Sides
Let your arms hang down at your sides. Tell her, "Sweetie, watch me." Ignore her if she sniffs your hands. When she looks at your face, praise her, "Yeah! Good girl!" and pop a treat in her mouth.

Arms Shoulder Height

Hold your arms straight out from your shoulders to each side. Tell her, "Sweetie, watch me." When she looks at your face, praise her, "Yeah! Good girl!" and pop a treat in her mouth.

Arms in Different Positions

Hold your arms in different positions—even one up and one down. Tell her, "Sweetie, watch me." When she looks at your face, praise her, "Yeah! Good girl!" and pop a treat in her mouth.

No Pulling Allowed

Ideally, when you walk your dog, she will walk nicely with you without pulling on the leash. Far too often, the dog leads the way, going this way and then that way, pulling hard. A dog who continually pulls hard or who lunges will hurt herself and her owner. It doesn't have to be this way; you can teach your dog to walk nicely with you.

Beware of using gadgets and tools to help teach your dog to walk nicely on the leash. There are no-pull harnesses, elastic leashes, leashes that squeak or whistle when the dog pulls, and a whole bunch of other things designed to make it easier to walk your dog. The problem with all of these is that they are not teaching the dog what she should be doing—walking on the leash without pulling. Instead the gadgets are simply a means of managing the situation. That is, if the dog pays any attention to them at all.

The first leash skill to be taught is called Let's Go. This exercise teaches your dog to walk nicely without pulling, while at the same time giving your dog the freedom of the leash. He can sniff, relieve himself, and relax as long as he doesn't pull. There are two techniques to teach this exercise.

Teaching Let's Go

Loose Leash Walking

With your dog on loose leash, tell her, "Sweetie, let's go," and begin walking. She can sniff, move around you, or walk ahead. You can decide how much leash she can have—4 feet or 6 feet—but be consistent. Don't give her 4 feet one day and 6 feet another day.

Be an Anchor

Should your dog dash ahead of you (or in any direction) and begin pulling, just stop walking. Hold the leash tightly and don't move. You can give a verbal interruption if you wish. When your dog stops pulling and turns to look at you, praise her.

Back to a Loose Leash

Once your dog has stopped pulling, then tell her, "Sweetie, let's go," and begin walking again. Praise her verbally, "Sweetie, good let's go. Yeah!" But don't be surprised if she pulls again; it will take practice.

Stop and Watch Me

If your dog lunges forward when you begin walking, stop and ask for a Watch Me. If she can't even do that, hold her by her collar and help her sit. While you're bent over, do a close Watch Me, praise her, and give her the treat. Repeat until she calms down.

Alternative Techniques

Turn Around

If your dog is good at the Watch Me but you have tried the Let's Go and your dog is still pulling, then it's time to try something else. When your dog pulls ahead, simply turn around and go another direction. Don't ask, coax, or warn your dog; just go. Don't yank your dog or try to make her do back flips—don't be angry. Catch her by surprise and walk away from her.

Praise Her

After you have turned and are walking in another direction, when she catches up to you, praise her, "Hi, Sweetie, good!" If she dashes past to pull, turn around again. After several of these surprise turns, she's going to be paying more attention to you. Praise her for that attention.

Change in Training Tools

Martingale Collar

If your dog is still pulling, it might be time to change training tools. For some dogs the martingale collar is a good choice. When the dog pulls, the collar will tighten slightly. You can then use a pop—not a yank or jerk—as you tell her, "Ack! No pull!" Then praise her when she responds. Teach her that the best thing she can do is walk with you.

Head Halter

If the dog pulls in a head halter, as her legs push forward and you hold the leash, her head won't be able to go forward with her body, and she will end up facing you. Praise her. Do not use a pop, yank, or jerk with the head halter. Follow your interruption of her forward momentum by showing her what to do.

Remember, whenever you interrupt behaviors you don't want to continue—such as pulling—you must teach your dog what you do want to happen in the future. An interruption creates a teaching moment.

A Leash Game

Keeping your dog focused on you can be hard. After all, you're with your dog a lot—but that squirrel is sure fun to chase! The dog behind the neighbor's gate is barking, too, and that's pretty interesting. But your success in teaching your dog not to pull is based on her desire to work with you and maintain a loose leash.

The leash game uses the skills you've been teaching your dog and turns them into a game. As you've seen previously, anything you teach your dog is more fun when you play a game than when you simply train and repeat things over and over.

To play the leash game you need a leash on your dog, some distractions, and some really special treats. Choose something your dog doesn't normally get—maybe some small pieces of last night's beef pot roast or steak or some brie cheese. Have a plastic bag of these treats and put them in your pocket for easy access.

Goal of the Game

The goal of this game is to help your dog follow you while you back away from her. You'll use your voice to praise and encourage her and the treat will reward her. As she gets better at following you, you're going to make it harder. As the game gets harder, the rewards will get better.

Back Away

Give your dog the entire length of the leash to move around. Hold one of those special treats in your other hand and let her sniff it. Then, without any verbal cues, begin backing away from your dog. If she follows you, praise her. After several steps, stop, have her sit, give her the treat, and repeat this exercise.

Curves and Turns

When your dog will follow you as you back up straight, then it's time to add some more fun. Back up in curves and add some corners. Back up to the right and then the left. Cheer your dog on, and when she catches up to you, pet her, give her a treat, and tell her what a wonderful dog she is!

More Challenges

If your dog masters curves and corners, then it's time to add some challenges. This time back away a few steps, then turn and walk forward but keep looking toward your dog so you can maintain eye contact. Walk faster, move in zigzag patterns, and dash to the right or left. Cheer your dog on when she stays with you.

Teaching Heel

Whereas the Let's Go is relaxed, the Heel is more formal. Rather than having freedom of the leash, when heeling, your dog will walk by your side and maintain that position.

A dog who is heeling nicely is a joy to behold. The dog walks by the left side, her shoulder by her owner's left leg, and maintains that position as they move forward together; the heel is wonderful teamwork.

That teamwork has to be built, however, as the Heel can be tough. But if you build it step by step, it can be done without too much difficulty.

The Heel starts with the Watch Me and attention game. If your dog isn't paying good attention to you, she won't be able to heel nicely and will continue to forge ahead and pull.

Go back and really focus on the Watch Me and attention game. Interrupt your dog when she gets distracted and use some great verbal praise and special treats when she is focused on you. Make paying attention to you extra special. Then work on the Let's Go leash skills and play the leash game.

Teaching the Heel

Begin in the Correct Position

Have your dog sit by your left side. Her shoulder and base of the neck should be next to your left leg. The position is correct if you can make a left turn and not trip over her. Hold the leash in your left hand and treats in your right. Bring your right hand across your body, let her sniff the treats and tell her, "Sweetie, watch me!"

Use Treat as Needed

As you walk forward, feel free to praise your dog when she's walking nicely. Don't keep the treat at your dog's nose all the time. Keep one in your hand—your dog knows it's there—and use it when you need it. If your dog gets distracted, then bring the treat back and repeat the Watch Me.

Stop, Sit, and Reward

After heeling a few steps, stop, sit your dog, and reward her. Heel requires a great deal of concentration; it's hard. Each time your dog sits, not only does she get rewards from you, but she can relax a moment. If she's getting tense or losing her concentration, then after a sit release her and let her relax a little more. Then repeat the exercise.

Add Distractions

When you and your dog are doing well with short walks forward, add some distractions. Walk forward, make right turns and left turns, and turn around and go back the way you started. Heel in a figure eight pattern around two trash cans. Ask your dog to heel in the neighborhood when the kids are coming home from school.

Using These Exercises

Leash skills are used all the time—whenever you go for a walk—so it's not difficult to use them. It is important to vary these skills, though, as heeling for every walk every day can be tough and not a lot of fun for you or your dog.

As you begin each walk, start with your dog in a heel. Your dog is probably excited to be going for a walk and may try to pull, but because the Heel is more controlled—she walks in a specific position—she can then calm herself and get herself under control.

After a couple of blocks, stop, have your dog sit, and as you begin to walk, tell her, "Sweetie, let's go." She can relax, sniff, and look around as long as she doesn't pull.

If some kids on skateboards or rowdy dogs are heading your direction, bring your dog back to a Heel. When they are gone she can go back to a Let's Go. Throw in a leash game here or there for fun. If you take her to the hardware store with you, have her heel. It will take some practice, but as you use these leash skills and your dog gets better with them, you'll discover which skill works better for you in various situations.

Chapter 13

Teaching Leave It

- Leave It means ignore it
- Keep your dog safe
- Many uses for Leave It

The Leave It exercise is one that can make living with your dog easier. Living with a dog requires some compromises, but that doesn't mean your dog can steal your food any time you step away from it. When you teach your dog that he needs to ignore certain things—including your food—then living with a dog becomes more enjoyable.

Teaching your dog to ignore some items will keep him safer. There are many things that are potentially dangerous to your dog both in your home and that can be encountered while out on walks. Trash cans with wrappers and bits of food and cupboards with cleaning supplies and other chemicals can cause problems. Then there are all those items we use regularly but that can be toxic to dogs such as cigarettes, makeup, and even chocolate.

The Leave It exercise can be used in the house, out in the yard, and even out in public. This is an easy exercise to teach, but it will require consistent repetition to build new habits. Frequently your dog will have no desire to ignore these interesting items. It's well worth the time and effort necessary to keep your dog safe.

Leave It

The Leave It exercise teaches your dog to ignore certain items when you tell him to ignore them. When you drop a piece of food to the floor, for example, you can tell your dog to ignore that piece of food. But your dog is not going to generalize immediately that every piece of dropped food should be ignored. Initially he will think that only that one piece of food is bad.

As you teach your dog and practice this exercise, over time he will begin to generalize. If he is told to ignore the kitchen trash can no matter what is in it, he will eventually realize that the kitchen trash can is never to be touched.

How long this process take depends on your dog. If he's a puppy (and mentally immature) it will take several months and perhaps as much as a year to become reliable. If you have a dog who has an established habit of stealing food or raiding the trash can, he will need several months of training to overcome this habit. An adult dog without bad habits and who is motivated to learn could accomplish this within a few weeks.

When teaching and practicing this exercise, always use a leash on your dog. If you don't have a leash on him, he could grab the item you're trying to teach him to ignore—especially if it's food—and then dash away with it.

Do not tell your dog to ignore something and then tell him he can have it. This is confusing to your dog.

Trade for Treats

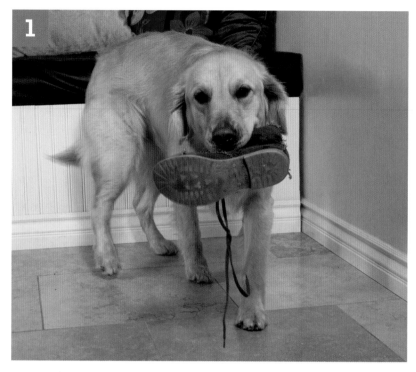

Build Cooperation

Before teaching your dog the Leave It exercise, it's important to teach your dog to bring items to you rather than run away with them. If you teach him that you aren't going to yell or otherwise make the situation worse, and you'll trade him a treat for the item, you will gain his cooperation. Then if he has something he shouldn't, you can get it away from him easily.

Offer a Treat

Practice this with an item your dog often takes such as a shoe or slipper. Without giving him permission, toss that slipper and let him get it. Then walk to where you normally keep the dog treats and get one, letting him see and hear you. Call his name and let him know you have a treat, "Sweetie, cookie!"

Give the Treat

As your dog comes to you for the treat, tell him, "Sweetie, give," as you hold out a treat with one hand and get ready to take the shoe. When he spits out the shoe, praise him, "Sweetie, thank you! Good to give!" Give him the treat. If he tries to dash away from you, step on the leash to stop him. Then repeat the exercise.

Praise, Pet, and Substitute

Once your dog has dropped the shoe and you've given him the treat, enthusiastically praise and pet him. After all, he's given up something he likes. Then take him to one of his toys and encourage him to play with this instead. Toss the toy, and praise him for chasing after it.

Teaching Leave It

Get Ready

With your dog on leash, have him sit by your left side. Hold the leash in your left hand and keep it short but not tight on your dog's neck; just a little bit of slack is good. Have something that's a temptation in your right hand. Half a peanut butter sandwich is great.

"Sweetie, Leave It"

Place the sandwich on the ground in front of your dog as you tell him, "Sweetie, leave it." If he tries to grab it, use the leash to stop him. Have him maintain the sit position. Then, using a training treat, get his attention and tell him, "Sweetie, watch me!" Praise him when he looks at you.

Wait a Few Seconds

Encourage your dog to watch you and ignore the treat by praising him when he looks at you. Don't say anything if he looks at the sandwich. Ask him to hold this position for 5 seconds in the beginning and then gradually increase the time to 30 to 45 seconds depending on your dog's concentration.

Turn Him Away

After a few seconds, turn him away from the sandwich, praise and pet him, and reach back to pick up the sandwich. Physically turn him away because if you praised him in his original position, he'd reach down and grab the sandwich. Turn him away from it before you pet him.

Using the Leave It

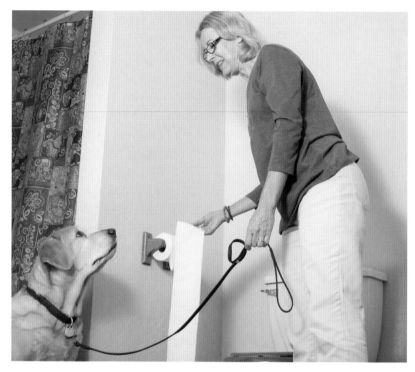

In the House

Every dog finds things that amuse him. Some dogs love to unroll the toilet paper while other dogs prefer to dig stuff out of trash cans. Some dogs like shoes or slippers while others focus on food. Choose one or two things your dog is attracted to and begin teaching Leave It with those. When those are well understood—usually a couple of weeks—then begin teaching using other items.

Your Daily Routine

Once your dog understands the Leave It, begin using it during your daily routine. Have a leash on your dog so you can follow through should he grab something, but otherwise go through some of your normal routines. Fix a meal and as you do so, drop a piece of food to the floor and tell your dog, "Sweetie, leave it." Praise him when he does.

Out in Public

When you're out for a walk and you approach some trash, dog feces that hasn't been picked up, or anything else you'd like your dog to avoid, tell him, "Sweetie, leave it! Watch me! Good!" Then walk on past it. Remember the Leave It tells him to ignore the item, and the Watch Me tells him what to do instead.

Expect the Unexpected

Things will grab your dog's attention at the oddest times. Perhaps on a walk you'll encounter a child's toy. Your dog can look at it, of course, but should he lunge for it, tell him to leave it and watch you. Help him do it using treats and your voice, and then walk on by. Praise him.

Part 4

Training Challenges

Training a puppy is not significantly different from training an adult dog. The puppy can be introduced to the basic obedience exercises; however, allowances must be made for the puppy's immaturity and short concentration span. It's especially important to keep the training fun for the puppy.

Things that dog owners consider to be problem behaviors—such as barking, digging, destructive chewing, and more—are natural behaviors to the dog. Remember this when trying to change or lessen them.

Once your dog has a good foundation of basic obedience skills, there's a lot more you both can do. Canine activities and sports are popular. The Canine Good Citizen program should be a goal for all dog owners. Agility competitions are great exercise and a lot of fun. Therapy dog volunteer work is rewarding for everyone. The joy of sharing your life with a dog is the companionship and laughter; doing more with your dog just multiplies that.

Chapter 14

Training Your Puppy

- Practice patience
- Lure and reward works for puppies
- Set up your puppy to succeed
- Socialization is vital

There is nothing quite as cute as a puppy. With rounded features, a fat tummy, clumsy paws, and big eyes, puppies of all breeds and mixes pull at our heartstrings. When you bring home your new puppy, your life will change. She's going to give you unconditional love, make you laugh, and sometimes frustrate you beyond belief.

Start training your puppy early, but keep the training sessions easy and very short. The lure and reward technique works as well for puppies as for dogs. The puppy's freedom needs to be restricted to help prevent problem behaviors. Supervision is more important for puppies because they don't have any knowledge whatsoever about what is safe and what isn't. Puppies will get into everything and chew on anything.

Socialization is an important part of raising a puppy. The best age for beginning your puppy's introduction to the world is between 12 and 16 weeks of age. The process should then continue through puppyhood and on into adulthood. Although this ongoing socialization is important, what happens at 3 and 4 months of age is the most vital.

Although many puppy owners understand that puppies need to meet people and other puppies during this socialization stage of life, there's more to it than that. The puppy needs to meet, see, hear, smell, and feel the various parts of her world in small amounts that won't frighten her.

Puppies Are Babies

Your puppy needs your protection, supervision, guidance, and—most importantly—affection. Puppies are helpless. They don't know how their world functions. If she's hungry how does she find food? Where does food come from? If she follows her nose she might find food scraps in the trash can, cat food in another room, or even the cat litter. She has no idea these things can be dangerous.

When your puppy was with her mother and littermates, if she was tired, lonely, chilly, or just needed company, she would cuddle up to them. She doesn't know who will take their place. If you have an older dog, she will snuggle up to him if he'll allow it. But this is the time to invite her to cuddle with you, too, so she learns she can look to you for comfort.

The important thing to remember as you begin to teach your puppy is that she is a baby. Take things slow, keep your communication with her clear, and spend the time bonding with her. She needs to learn many things, of course, but bonding and developing a relationship with her is also important.

Everything Is New

If you stop by the pet supply store on the way home one day and choose a new toy for your puppy, don't be surprised if she's startled when you toss it to her. Everything in this world is new to your puppy. Take the new toy and wiggle it like a critter while you encourage her with a happy voice, "Sweetie, it's a toy! Yeah!" When she starts to move toward it, praise her in a happy tone of voice and if she pounces on it, let her run off with it.

Each day you'll see your puppy gain confidence and it's fun to watch. But at the same time, she has to learn what she's allowed to investigate, what she can play with, what is safe to eat, and what she has to ignore. Everything is new.

Keep her close to you and limit her freedom significantly to prevent problems. Then use your training skills to teach her.

Patience Is Needed

Raising a puppy requires a lot of patience. Puppies have housetraining accidents, bite with their sharp teeth, cry when they're lonely, and wake you up in the middle of the night. As babies, they react to everything that happens to them in a dramatic fashion.

Puppies also disrupt your life and your household. They need attention and training. You need to organize your routine around the puppy's needs. Be patient, however, as this stage of life won't last forever.

Think of the Future

As you raise your puppy and teach her, have in mind a vision of what you would like her to be as an adult. Teach her the rules and manners you'd like her to have when she's all grown up. Make the training appropriate for her age, of course, but raise her as you would like her to grow up.

Far too many puppy owners assume that puppies will outgrow bad behaviors, but that isn't true. Puppies (and dogs) repeat behaviors that are rewarding to them. For example, if raiding the trash can gains them some food tidbits, they will continue to do it.

Therefore decide what's important to you and what isn't. Decide on the household rules and social manners you would like your future adult dog to know and start implementing them during puppyhood. Prevent or interrupt behaviors you don't want to continue.

The Process Is the Same

The process of training a puppy is much like that of training a dog. Your puppy's brain is mature enough to learn, and in fact she's learning all the time. She knows when you put on certain clothes and shoes, for example, that you'll be going to work; and although she has no concept of work, she does know you'll be gone for a while. This is a great time to begin teaching her.

The primary difference between the training sessions for a puppy and a dog is that puppies have a very short concentration span. A nice training session for an adult dog might be 15 minutes in length, whereas one for a puppy under 4 months of age is best limited to 3 or 4 minutes at a time. From 4 to 6 months of age, a session can last 6 to 8 minutes at a time.

Several short sessions per day are much better than trying to force your puppy to concentrate for one longer session. Even if your puppy were able to concentrate for a longer session each day, her retention of what is being taught would be low. A two minute session before breakfast, another one at noon, one before dinner, and one before bedtime would work wonderfully.

Lure and Reward Works Well

As with adult dogs, there are many different ways to teach puppies. Most will learn how to respond to clicker training techniques very well early in puppyhood. However, because the training must be easy for the owner as well as the puppy, lure and reward techniques will be taught in this chapter, too.

Puppies are continually growing and have great appetites; therefore, puppies usually aren't as picky about training treats as adult dogs can be. The most important thing is to make the training treats tiny; especially if you have a small or toy breed puppy. You don't want your puppy to become full halfway through the training session, nor do you want your puppy to get fat.

Again, as with dogs, choose healthy treats that smell good. Keep in mind the sense of smell is more important to puppies and dogs than is taste.

Keep Your Puppy Safe

Limit Freedom Even More

It's important to limit all dogs' freedom during training, but it's even more important for puppies. Not only are puppies unaware of things that are potentially dangerous, they're also curious enough to try and get into cupboards and other places where dangers are common. Puppy-proofing the house and yard are important, but the puppy's access to these things must be prevented.

Be Careful Everywhere

By keeping your puppy on leash—or restricted with a crate, baby gate, or exercise pen—you can help keep her safe no matter where she is or what you're doing. You don't want to isolate your puppy; she needs to spend time with you. But since she doesn't understand what's safe and what isn't, it's up to you to show her.

Prevent Bad Habits

If you limit your puppy's freedom early in life, she will never learn to chase cars or cats. If she never raids the trash cans, she won't know there are tasty food wrappers inside. By limiting her freedom, you are preventing her from learning potentially rewarding yet dangerous habits.

This Can Be Fun

Keeping your puppy close to you or limiting her freedom with a crate, baby gate, or exercise pen can be annoying. But it's also a great time to develop a relationship with your puppy; to bond with her. Pet your puppy often, talk to her, practice her training skills, and play with her.

Teaching Your Puppy

Interrupt and Redirect

Although your puppy's freedom needs to be limited, there are times when she can be loose in the house without a leash. These moments need to be supervised so you can use them as teaching moments. Interrupt any actions you don't want repeated, and then redirect her.

How to Interrupt

What you do to interrupt a puppy's actions depends on how close you are to the puppy at that moment. If you're within a step and an arm's reach, put a treat in front of the puppy's nose and call her name. Use the treat to turn her away from what you want her to ignore.

Second Technique

If you aren't within arm's reach, then make a noise to get her attention. Clang a pot lid, drop the book you were reading, quack like a duck, or clap your hands. Don't try to scare her; just make enough noise to distract her. As you're doing this, walk toward her so you can continue to turn her away from that item.

Redirect Puppy

Once you have interrupted the action you don't want the puppy to pursue, you then need to encourage her to do something else. Wiggle a toy in front of her and tell her, "Sweetie, get the toy!" Praise her when she pounces on it. Toss her favorite ball and praise her for running after it.

Help Your Puppy Succeed

The best way to help your puppy grow up to be a well-behaved dog is to teach her what you want her to do. By teaching good behaviors and turning them into habits, she'll be less likely to develop bad behaviors.

If you don't want your puppy napping on the sofa or chairs in the living room, provide an open crate or a doggy bed placed near where you normally relax. Give her a treat or something to chew on when she relaxes there.

Preventing actions you don't want is also important. If you don't want your puppy up on the sofa, for example, don't ever let her jump up there. Should she jump up one day, interrupt her, put her off the sofa, and praise her when all four paws are on the floor.

As with dogs, puppies will repeat actions that are self-rewarding. If she jumps up on the sofa and one day you give in, snuggle with her, rub her tummy, and tell her how cute she is, then that becomes a reward. She's going to jump up again and expect to have a good time with you.

To help your puppy succeed, keep all three of these suggestions in mind. Just following one of the suggestions won't work; all three are a part of the teaching process.

The Basic Exercises

Teach the basic obedience exercises as well as household rules. Not only will the basic obedience exercises help you teach your puppy the household rules, but the training will also help you establish two-way communication with your puppy. You'll be watching her as you teach her, so you'll be able to see when she's confused or when she understands.

Training will help you build a relationship with your puppy, too. As you communicate with your puppy better, and as she learns you'll be fair with her, her trust in you will increase. The bond between the two of you will grow.

Your puppy is able to learn Sit, Down, Stay, Come, and to walk nicely on a leash. Teach these skills as they were explained in previous chapters, and keep the training sessions short.

Socialization

Socializing a puppy is the process of introducing your puppy to the world she lives in. By methodically and gently showing your puppy that the world is not a scary place, she will grow up confident and secure.

Puppies who are not well socialized tend to be fearful adult dogs. Adult dogs who are worried about everything are more apt to run away when frightened or bite when they can't run away.

Socialization isn't difficult but it may be disruptive to your daily routine. Unfortunately, it is a necessary part of puppyhood and you can't make up for it later. So no matter how busy you are, you have to take the time to do it.

The Best Age to Socialize

Wise breeders begin socialization when the puppies are 3 weeks old. Although the puppies cannot meet other dogs and people (other than family members) now, they can be introduced to different surfaces under their paws and simple toys. A cardboard oatmeal container, a piece of fleece blanket, and lumps and bumps under the blanket are all simple ways to socialize young puppies.

Once you bring your puppy home, she can begin learning all about her new home. You can intro-duce her to the sights, sounds, and smells in the house and backyard. After a few days at home, then invite neighbors and extended family over to meet her—a couple of people at a time so you don't overwhelm her.

Socialization to the world outside her home—as well as to other people, puppies, and friendly adult dogs—should begin between 12 and 16 weeks of age, after she's had at least 2 sets of vac-cinations. The timing can vary depending on what vaccinations she was given and at what ages. Check with your veterinarian to be sure.

Socializing Safely

As you introduce your puppy to new things, think about how a new experience might frighten her. Take things slowly, and minimize other stimuli, so you don't overwhelm her.

Learning about new things should be matter-of-fact. Talk to her, "Let's go, Sweetie," as you both walk on a different surface, for example. If she wants to sniff the new floor, that's fine. If she's hesitant, show her a treat and encourage her to walk forward. Praise her and pop a treat in her mouth when she does.

Introducing New Things

Your puppy needs to learn all about the world she lives in, but you don't need—or want—to introduce them all at once. Instead, try to show her one new thing each day. Make each introduction fun and exciting, use your voice to encourage and praise, and have some really good treats as lures and rewards.

For example, the next time you empty the kitchen trash can, take out the trash and before you put the new trash bag in the can, drop it to the floor and invite your puppy to investigate it. When she's comfortable, flap it a little. Then drop a treat on it so she needs to step on the bag to get the treat. Praise her.

Make a List

If it helps you introduce one new thing each day, make a list of the things she needs to get to know. Of course, every home is different so look around your home, yard, and garage.

Some items you can introduce your puppy to:

- **Kitchen:** The sound of the garbage disposal, dishwasher, ice machine, the broom and dustpan, a plastic grocery bag, a crumpled paper bag, as well as pans and lids.

- **Rest of the house:** The vacuum cleaner, washing machine and dryer, the dust mop, doors opening and closing, a mirror, glass doors and windows, kids' toys, remote control toys, the bathtub and shower, hair dryer, and a ceiling fan.

- **Your stuff:** An umbrella, a rain coat, a hat, a scarf, gloves, different shoes and boots.

- **In the neighborhood:** The garbage truck, a motorcycle driving past, bicycles, skateboards, a baby stroller, and little kids' tricycles.

What else? Do you have a sewing machine? A compressor in the garage? If you use something and see your puppy begin to react, stop and introduce her to it.

People and Pets

Your puppy needs to meet other animals and people. Keep the meetings upbeat and friendly. Don't allow anyone to frighten your puppy, get too rough with her, finger fight with her, or do anything else that might leave a bad memory.

She should meet:

- People of all ages, sizes, and ethnic backgrounds. Introduce her to one or two people at a time and remove her from the situation if people are too rough.

- Puppies close to her age who are vaccinated and healthy.

- Friendly, healthy adult dogs who are known to be gentle with puppies. Do not take her to the dog park where unknown dogs might be too rough or might not be healthy.

- Cats and kittens—again preferably ones known to be friendly to dogs.

- Rabbits, ferrets, turtles, tortoises, a dog-friendly horse, and other pets.

Use common sense here. If a neighbor's dog seems to be unfriendly, don't introduce your puppy even if the neighbor swears he's okay. Being a little overprotective is fine.

Stimulate Her Senses

Another part of socialization and puppy training is helping her learn through her senses of sight, sound, smell, and touch. These are important to her—especially smell and hearing—as she learns just as much about her world through her senses as we do.

Expose her to different walking surfaces like grass, concrete, sand, dirt, bark, and a small wooden bridge if you can find one. Walk her on tile, carpet, rubber matting, and a slippery floor. Take her for a ride in an elevator and make it fun for her when she feels the floor moving under her.

Take her to places that smell different. Walk her outside a local fish restaurant or the harbor where there are some fishing boats.

Take a look around your neighborhood and city. Look with fresh eyes. What are you taking for granted that will be new to your puppy?

Cautions

Socialize your puppy gradually—ideally introducing one new thing a day. If you expose her to too much too soon you can overwhelm her, and that's just as bad as not socializing her in the first place. Too much is scary.

When introducing her to people, have one or two people at a time meet her. If people—even kids—gang up on her, pick her up and have the people move away. If you're introducing her to another animal, and that animal is getting too excited or seems unfriendly, move your puppy away.

Don't ever let things get out of hand. Maintain control of the situation when introducing her to people and animals. Pick her up and take her away if things are getting too exciting, rowdy, or scary.

Chapter 15

Preventing Problem Behaviors

- Exercise for mental and physical health
- Keep the brain active
- Diet affects behavior
- You and your dog are a team

The vast majority of behaviors that dog owners consider to be problems are natural behaviors to your dog. Rather than attempting to stop an undesired behavior, then, it is often more effective to redirect your dog's physical and mental energy.

A tired dog is less likely to get into trouble than a dog full of energy who hasn't had regular exercise. But be careful not to exercise your dog too much—yes, that *is* possible. Find the right balance for your dog.

Your dog's brain also needs to be exercised. Obedience training, trick training, games, and other means of helping your dog think and use his brain will also burn energy. In fact, you may notice that after playing some brain games your dog is more tired than when he chased a ball for the same period of time.

What your dog eats can also affect his behavior. Some dogs have food sensitivities, and eating a food with those specific ingredients can cause changes in behavior. These dogs have trouble concentrating and difficulty retaining what they've learned.

How much and how well your dog was socialized as a puppy is often reflected in an adult dog's behavior. Some behaviors are fairly typical for dogs who haven't been well socialized.

Dogs do things for a variety of reasons. Thankfully, behaviors you consider to be less than ideal can often be changed or lessened.

Physical Exercise Is Important

Healthy dogs of all ages can benefit from daily exercise. Running, jumping, playing, and swimming keep the body strong and functioning well.

With obesity becoming far too common in our dogs, it is especially important to encourage exercise. Diet is important, too; what and how much you feed your dog are also an important part of weight control. But a dog who gets regular exercise will be far less likely to become obese.

A lack of exercise can lead to behavior problems because an excess of energy will cause him to look for ways to amuse himself. A puppy or adolescent in particular will be bouncing off the furniture; chewing on anything that will fit into his mouth; and pacing, barking, and digging in the back yard.

How much exercise is needed depends on the individual dog, the breed, the age, and state of his health. A 9 month old Australian shepherd, for example, will be happy with a 30 minute walk, a 15 minute game of fetch, and a chance to chase another dog around the yard for another 15 minutes. A 9 month old dachshund, however, will be happy with ¼ that much exercise.

A Tired Dog Will Nap

One of the best reasons for exercise, besides improving your dog's overall physical health, is that a tired dog is going to be happy to take a nap afterward. A tired dog is not going to look for ways to get into trouble or for things to destroy.

You can use this to your advantage by timing your dog's exercise sessions. If your dog is not happy when you leave for work in the morning, get up 15 minutes earlier and take your dog for a run or a brisk walk. Throw the ball or his favorite toy for him. Then get ready for work. When you leave, he'll be more likely to snooze, and as a result he'll be far less fretful.

What you do to exercise your puppy depends on your likes and abilities as well as those of your dog. Most dogs love to run, for example, but if you aren't a runner, don't try to run with your dog. Not only will you probably hate it, you might hurt yourself. Plus, because you don't like it, you won't keep it up. Choose things that you and your dog both like.

Exercise Ideas

Go for a Walk

Most dog owners like to walk their dogs, and this is something that any healthy dog can do. The speed and length of the walk can be tailored to the age, health, and ability of the dog. A 3-month-old Chihuahua, for example, only needs to walk a couple of blocks while a young adult Labrador retriever can walk 5 miles.

Out for a Run

If your dog is an adult, healthy, and physically sound—and you are equally healthy and sound—then the two of you may enjoy a daily run. Start easy so your dog toughens his muscles and paws. Use your training skills to teach him to run in the Heel position next to you. If he runs in front of you or zigzags back and forth, you could trip over him.

Retrieving Games

Chasing a flying disc or a tennis ball is the world's best game for many dogs. It's also great exercise. When combined with the fact that you can often play in your own backyard, this is almost the perfect exercise. The only drawback is that puppies shouldn't be jumping high for the thrown toy due to the risk of hurting themselves, so throw the ball low for them.

Play is Fun and Exercise

Playing with your dog is great fun but it can also be good exercise. Dog owners have often been told not to play tug games, but when played correctly they're absolutely fine and are good exercise. Hide and seek in the backyard is good fun. Hide and call your dog so he has to find you. Have fun with your dog.

Exercising a Puppy

Puppies and adolescents need daily exercise but should not be pushed (nor allowed) to exercise as much or as hard as an adult dog. Small dogs under 1 year of age, medium-size dogs under about 18 months, and large dogs under 2 years of age are still considered puppies or adolescents.

Puppies grow rapidly, and as a result are clumsy and uncoordinated. Also, the growth plates on their bones (the ends of the long bones) haven't closed. Repeated impacts from running on hard surfaces, jumping, and other strenuous exercise can damage those growth plates and hence the bones. If you have any questions about your puppy's growth plates, when they will close, and how much exercise your puppy should get, talk to your veterinarian.

Adult Dogs

As long as your adult dog is healthy, he should be allowed to play and exercise as long as he wants to and is comfortable. That means, of course, that your dog's body conformation, fitness level, and physical abilities are taken into consideration.

Dogs with shortened muzzles, such as pugs and bulldogs, cannot breathe well and should not be pushed to exercise. They also need to have all physical activity in the morning, evening, or inside in the air conditioning.

Short-legged, long-backed dogs, such as dachshunds and corgis, are prone to back problems. They should not jump up and down off of objects, nor should they jump up after thrown toys.

If you have any doubts, worries, or concerns about what your dog should or should not do, talk to your veterinarian before you begin any exercise program for your dog. Then for all dogs, begin easily and allow your dog time to get used to the program.

Don't Overdo It

Although exercise is good for your dog, physically and mentally, you can overdo it. The most common thing that owners do is to play or exercise with the dog until he hurts himself. Many dogs will play ball until their paws bleed or jump until their muscles are sore. Dog owners need to be smarter than the dog and know when to stop him.

Some dogs will also get mentally overstimulated, especially when playing certain games or sports. If you find that your dog likes one particular game so much that he can't control his barking, he begins screaming or howling in excitement, or he begins jumping on the other dogs because he can't control himself, then remove him from the game.

Tire the Brain, Too

The vast majority of dog breeds were originally designed to work for mankind; they had a job to do. Although most dogs today are companions, many retain their working instincts. A dog who was bred to do a job and is now simply a pet with no sense of purpose, no job to do, and who is left alone for hours each day is going to get into trouble. He may dig up the backyard, try to escape from the yard, or will bark any time he hears a noise.

Exercising your dog's brain as well as his body will help prevent some of these behavior problems. There are many ways to exercise his brain, and obedience training is certainly one of them. A daily training session is great. Additional training, like trick training, is fun and also helps your dog use his brain.

Some brain exercises can be used when your dog is home alone; you can give him a food dispensing toy when you leave the house, for example. Other brain games are designed for the two of you to play together; or you can make a game out of some training exercises.

When Your Dog Is Home Alone

The Kong

Kong toys, which are made by the Kong Company, are hard rubber toys that look like a hollow snowman. They are fun toys to toss; they bounce every which way. However, they are best when stuffed with peanut butter, cheese, banana, dog kibble, or other foods. A stuffed Kong can keep your dog occupied for a while as you leave for work.

Kong Wobbler

The Wobbler, also made by the Kong Company, can be used to dispense treats, but it can also hold an entire meal. If your dog gets worried or overly excited when you leave for work, give him his meal in the Wobbler. He won't even notice you leaving because he'll be working to get his breakfast out of the toy.

More Food Dispensing Toys

You can buy several toys and alternate them from day to day, or find a couple your dog really enjoys and just use those. Make sure the toy is big enough that your dog won't choke on it yet small enough he can manipulate it. It should be sturdy enough that he doesn't chew it up, too.

Environmental Enrichment

In hot weather, freeze a bucket of water with slices of apples, carrots, and dog biscuits mixed in; give it to your dog outside. Or, before you leave for work, hide some treats in the house or the backyard and encourage your dog to find them.

Brain Games to Play Together

Nina Ottosson Toys

Nina Ottosson began creating brainteaser toys for dogs in 1990 so that dogs—with their owners' help—could have fun while learning to solve puzzles. Her games are rated from easy to difficult; in any given game the dog may need to pull open drawers, flip something over, push, or turn something. When the puzzle is solved, the dog gets a treat.

Other Brain Games

With the success of the Ottosson toys, several companies are now making brainteaser toys. Some are made of wood and others plastic, but the goal is the same. The dog and owner work together to solve the puzzle so the dog can find the treat. While the dog solves the puzzle, you make sure your dog doesn't get too frustrated and give up.

The Flower Pot Game

This game requires your dog to use his scenting abilities as well as his problem solving abilities. Ask your dog to sit, then invert three small plastic flower pots in front of him. Place a treat under one. Encourage him to find the treat. When he noses the right flower pot, praise him and let him have the treat. As he gets more confident, let him knock the flower pot over.

Practice Push-Ups

Brains and Energy

A push-up consists of a Sit to a Down and back up to a Sit. This repetitive exercise requires your dog to think, to follow your verbal cues, and to use up some energy. If you cheer him on as he does it, it's also a game. Ask your dog to sit, drop his leash to the floor, and have a really good treat in your hand.

Sit to Down

Using the treat in front of your dog's nose, tell him, "Sweetie, down," and encourage him to follow the treat down. Praise him as he's moving. As he learns the game, begin working toward a fast down from the sit. To do that you can increase your verbal praise when he's moving quickly. A higher value treat also helps.

From Down Back Up

As soon as your dog's elbows touch the floor, start moving the treat back up. You want to bring your dog back up to the sit position, so tell him, "Sweetie, sit." If your dog is a little hesitant, encourage him verbally and use a tiny bit of pressure upward with the leash or with your hand on his collar.

Back in the Sit

When your dog is back in the sit position, praise, pet him, and give him the treat. As you practice and he's moving down and back up willingly, then have him do three push-ups before rewarding him, then four, then two. Make the rewards sporadic but enthusiastic.

Food Affects Behavior

What your dog eats can create changes in his behavior. We know that what we eat or drink can change our behavior; alcohol, of course, and caffeine are known to cause changes in what we do or say. But also high-sugar foods can cause hyperactivity in some people—especially some children—while favorite foods can comfort us.

With dogs, foods high in cereal grains (rice, wheat, corn, etc.) can create a type of hyperactivity. Puppies are usually more susceptible than adult dogs, but it's been seen in both. These dogs generally have a period of high activity within an hour after eating which is then followed by a nap; a sugar high followed by a crash.

In addition, these dogs often have trouble concentrating. This can result in training difficulties, including an inability to retain what is being taught. These dogs often do better eating a diet that is higher in meats, with carbohydrates that include fruits (apples, bananas, papayas) and tubers (sweet potatoes, carrots) rather than cereal grains.

Another food-related behavior problem concerns high-protein diets. Dogs who have a tendency toward aggressive behavior can become more aggressive when eating high-protein diets. This does not mean meat makes dogs aggressive; far from it. Dogs are carnivores and need to eat meats. But a dog who already shows aggressive behavior may escalate those behaviors when eating a high-protein food.

What is important to know is that just as food can cause changes in our behavior, it can also do so with our dogs. If you change foods and see changes in your dog, take a second look at the food. Or, if your dog is already having some behavior issues, that, too, might be a reason to look closer at what your dog is eating.

The better-quality dog foods do tend to cost more than the lesser-quality foods. However cost of the food should not be the qualifying factor for choosing it. Read the list of ingredients.

Look at the Label

Don't use advertisements or celebrity endorsements to choose your dog's food. Instead, take a look at the label—specifically the ingredients. The ingredients are listed, by weight, from the heaviest to the lightest. Look for a meat species name. Other ingredients may be fruits, vegetables, and tubers.

Ideally, you want a good quality meat to be the first ingredient. If it is listed by the species name—chicken or beef—then that is the species used. However, if the label says "meat meal" or "meat and bone meal," then a combination of species has probably been used. Avoid these foods; you really don't have any idea what is in them. These foods are considered lesser quality.

If the meat is listed as chicken (or beef or other animal) "by-products" or "by-product meal," that could be a good quality ingredient or a significantly lesser quality ingredient. Unfortunately by-products can contain a variety of body parts and one batch may be better than another.

If your dog is prone to allergies, is sensitive to some foods, or if you suspect he may be having behavior problems associated with the food he's eating, choose a food with one meat and one carbohydrate. There are many on the market. There are even many dog foods with unique proteins such as duck, venison, rabbit, or even kangaroo. The carbohydrate is often potato or sweet potato. It is much easier to pinpoint a problem with limited ingredients.

If You Make a Change

If you decide to change your dog's food, make any dietary changes gradually over several weeks. Abrupt changes can cause gastrointestinal upsets, including severe diarrhea.

A good rule to follow is to feed ¼ of the new food and ¾ of your dog's old food for a week. Then ½ and ½ for a week followed by ¾ of the new food and ¼ of the old food for a third week. Following this transition period, your dog should be ready to eat just the new food.

Changes in your dog's health as well as his behavior will take time. A few weeks after completely changing over to a new food, you may see less hyperactivity after eating, or less aggression. His coat may be shinier. Food-related changes are slow to show up, so be patient.

Talk to Your Veterinarian

If you have questions about what your dog is eating, talk to your veterinarian. She'll be able to discuss her thoughts on nutrition and perhaps give you some suggestions.

Not all veterinarians study nutrition in great detail, however, so don't be surprised if she refers you to a veterinarian who specializes in nutrition. If she feels your dog's behavior is caused by more than what he's eating, she may refer you to a behaviorist. Take advantage of these referrals; after all, the more you know the better.

Socialization

Dogs are social creatures and their mental health requires regular exposure to the world around them. The importance of socialization cannot be emphasized enough, especially with regard to your dog's mental health.

Dogs who have not been socialized and dogs who were socialized as puppies but are isolated as adults are at a high risk of developing behavior problems. These could range from destructive behavior to barking, or fearfulness and biting.

That said, simply turning your dog loose at a dog park is not always good socialization. You don't know who the dogs are, whether they have been vaccinated or are healthy, and how they act towards other dogs. Far too many dog fights—some with tragic results—occur at dog parks.

Instead, socialization—both in puppyhood and on into adulthood—needs to be carefully guided. As your puppy grows up, continue the exposure to other dogs, animals, people, places and things.

Don't Isolate Your Dog

It's a fact of life that many dogs are left home alone for hours each day. Although dogs and their owners might prefer that the owner works at home, it's rarely possible. But just because the dog needs to be left alone doesn't mean the dog has to be isolated or lonely.

Exercise is a great stress reliever, so it will help if your dog gets good exercise each day. Taking your dog for a walk before you leave for work will use up energy and give him time away from the house and backyard.

What is most important, though, is to make sure that when you get home from work, you and your dog break from your normal routine. Go to the hardware store where your dog will be welcome. Walk where other people and their dogs like to walk. Have a picnic dinner at the local park or eat on the patio of an outdoor café. Visit friends who have friendly dogs.

Wisely Socialize

Sometimes dog owners feel that getting a second dog will absolve them of the need to continue socializing their dog. Although a second dog will be someone to play with, this new dog will simply become a member of the dog's family. This isn't socialization.

Although socialization for puppies always includes introducing the puppy to sights, sounds, smells, and other things around the house and neighborhood, continuing socialization for an adult dog is getting away from the house. So change your schedule if need be, leash your dog, and get away from the house.

You're a Team

Sharing your life with a dog is a wonderful thing. Dogs provide us with companionship, affection, security, and so much more. Dogs help us maintain better mental health, so it's only fair that we help them in the same way.

For dogs to be mentally healthy, they need several things: physical exercise, mental stimulation, socialization, playtime, and games. But most importantly, our dogs need us.

Dogs are social animals who need people. Studies have shown that dogs raised without people never adapt to life with people. Those dogs also tend to be fearful and aggressive.

The best way to describe dog ownership is to consider the dog and owner a team. Living and working together in harmony sounds clichéd, but it's true.

Remember Your Goals

Your goal of having a well-trained, well-loved canine companion is a good one. Keep this in mind as you raise, train, and live with your dog. Keep this in mind, too, as you work to prevent problem behaviors, or to change behaviors your dog might already have.

Without these goals, it may seem like an awful lot of work to change a behavior problem. This is especially true if you need to make some changes in your own life, such as adjusting your schedule or taking the dog out for training or socializing after work when you'd much rather relax at home.

Your goals, however, give you something to work toward. If you need a reminder, post your goals somewhere prominent. The refrigerator is the perfect place for many people.

Be Consistent

Consistency is important. When teaching your dog the basic obedience exercises and then implementing them around the house and out in public, your dog needs to know these exercises are not optional.

If you are inconsistent about teaching and using the Sit, then your dog won't reliably sit for petting. He may sit when one person greets him but then jump up on someone else. Consistency in all of your dog's training is vital.

Family Unity

If you and your dog live alone, then this section doesn't apply to you. However, if you and your dog live with other family members or roommates, then share this section with everyone.

Family unity is important to making sure your dog understands what is required of him. If some people require the dog to sit for petting but others encourage the dog to jump up, then the dog will be confused.

Ideally, have a family meeting and discuss the goals for the dog. Talk about how to achieve those goals. Discuss any misgivings, dislikes, or misunderstandings. Come up with a vocabulary that everyone will use and post that on the refrigerator.

Chapter 16

Addressing Problem Behaviors

- Understanding why dogs do things
- Changing individual behaviors
- Using training to help
- Applying the changes

Your dog may have a few behaviors that you don't like and would like to change. Perhaps she grabs your hand with her mouth to drag you to the dog treat jar. Maybe she jumps up on the kids when they come home from school and when she's bored she dumps the kitchen trash can.

These are problem behaviors as far as you're concerned, but they aren't problems to your dog. They are natural actions for her. She uses her mouth to manipulate the world because paws don't always work as well as she'd like. She jumps up to greet people face to face. And when the kitchen trash can smells good, it's self-rewarding to hunt for goodies in it. Unfortunately for dogs, they are living in our world, so some of their natural behaviors are not appreciated by people.

Understanding why dogs do what they do can give you more insight in what's going on. Then you can prevent the problem as much as realistically possible.

Your training skills can help, often by teaching a replacement action. If your dog is sitting to greet people, for example, she's not jumping on them. Training can also teach your dog self-control, which helps many problem behaviors.

This chapter goes over ways to manage, control, or reduce the most common problem behaviors. If your dog has a problem that's not listed here, you can adapt these techniques to address it.

Jumping on You

Dogs who know each other will greet each other face to face. A younger dog will semi-crouch and will come up under an older dog's muzzle to lick the muzzle. This is a normal greeting routine that happens all the time between friendly dogs.

Many experts believe this is why dogs jump up on people. A dog who is happy her owner is home will jump up to greet her owner face to face. Others feel that dogs jump up so the owner's hands can touch them.

Unfortunately a dog can do a great deal of harm by jumping up on people. Jumping on a toddler, young child, or an elderly person can knock them down. Claws can rip clothes or scratch skin. A dog who jumps up as the owner is bending over can give a black eye or a broken nose. Jumping on people is a problem.

Preventing the Problem

The easiest way to stop your dog from jumping on you is to tell your dog to sit and then help her do it. The Sit is the first obedience exercise you taught your dog and is the one that helps teach her self-control.

To help control jumping, it's important that you greet your dog with empty hands. If you have a load of laundry to bring in the house or you've got tools in your hands for a household repair project, walk in the house first with empty hands so you can help her sit. Then make another trip to bring in your things.

Making a Change

When you have your dog sit for everything she wants—from petting to treats to her meals—she learns to control herself and hold that sit position. In the beginning, you'll have to help her by holding her collar, but with practice she'll be able to do it without your intervention. Always reward her in the Sit.

Don't wait until your dog jumps on you to react. Instead, each and every time your dog looks as if she is going to jump, or in situations when you know she usually does jump, help her sit. Then give her the attention she wants by praising and petting her.

Mistakes to Avoid

Don't knee your dog! One of the most common techniques used to stop jumping is kneeing the dog in the chest as she jumps. Don't ever do this. Your femur is the biggest bone in your body and by kneeing her in the chest you risk severely hurting her.

Don't turn your back to your dog when she's trying to jump up on you. This creates frustration in many dogs who are jumping for attention; owners have been bitten in the back of the legs, the buttocks, and even in the upper body. Face your dog and then help her sit.

Jumping on Other People

Dogs jump on other people for the same reasons they jump on their owners. Your dog might get overexcited when guests come to the house and will jump on them as they come in the front door. Or perhaps your dog will jump on your neighbors when you're talking out in the front yard.

In any case, a jumping dog can cause the same problems when jumping on other people as she does when she jumps on you. People could be knocked down or scratched, and clothes can be ruined.

Unfortunately, if your dog hurts someone or damages their belongings when she jumps on them, you are liable for her actions. That could be quite serious, especially if someone is hurt.

Preventing the Problem

The best way to prevent your dog from jumping on other people is to make sure she has a leash on when she's going to be greeting other people. Without a leash, you will have little to no control of her when she wants to jump up.

Your guests and other people who may want to pet her are not going to help you control your dog. They want to greet her and spoil her, not try to enforce rules. You don't want them to enforce the rules, anyway, as they might not do what you'd prefer them to do. They might knee her in the chest, grab her paws, or use any variety of outdated techniques.

Other guests will be offended by your jumping dog and will be trying to avoid her leaping paws. They might also be brushing the dirt and mud off their clothes or protecting their kids. It's hard to remember but not everyone loves dogs.

So, when guests ring your doorbell, call out to them, "Hold on and let me leash the dog." (If you're out on a walk your dog is on a leash already.) Then with the leash on her, you can teach her.

Making a Change

Use the Leash

Inside the house or outside, make sure your dog is on a leash when she's going to greet someone. The leash helps you control her actions so you teach her what you want her to do. Without the leash, she'll be dancing, bounding, and jumping in excitement. Trying to control her then is impossible.

Have Her Sit

Ask your friend to wait a minute before petting your dog. If your friend is resistant, tell her that you're trying to teach your dog manners. Then you can ask your dog to sit and even help her sit if she's overly excited. Keep one hand on your dog's collar to keep her in the sit position.

Help Her Hold Still

Once your dog is sitting and your hand is on her collar to help her control herself, then invite your friend to pet your dog. Should your dog pop up, interrupt her, ask your friend to stop petting, and have her sit again. Then let your friend pet her again.

Reward Her in the Sit

After your friend has greeted your dog and steps back, then you need to pet and reward your dog. Your rewards are far more important to her than anyone else's, so tell her what a wonderful dog she is. If she tried to jump and you had to help her back into the sit position, that's okay.

Barking Too Much

Do you find yourself yelling at your dog to shut up? Have neighbors complained—or nicely commented—that there is a lot of barking when you're not home? Too much barking is a fairly common problem.

Dogs bark for a variety of reasons. If your dog is watchful and protective of your home and yard, she may bark when people come up to the house. If your dog is overly watchful, she might bark anytime she sees or hears anyone. Dogs bark at the mail truck as well as any delivery trucks. These barks tend to be loud, fierce, and usually stop when the person or truck goes away.

Dogs also bark when they're bored. These barks usually sound bored and are repetitive; the same sound over and over. A worried dog left outside may bark shrilly in a frantic tone of voice.

As you can see, dogs bark for many reasons. Just as people speak to communicate, so do dogs. They're just speaking a different language.

Preventing the Problem

It may take some detective work on your part to determine why your dog is barking. You might need to go through the motions of leaving for work, drive down the street and walk back. Without your dog hearing, seeing, or smelling you, wait for the barking.

Once you've determined what is going on you can work to prevent it. Can you change where you leave your dog during the day? Will some extra exercise in the morning help her sleep while you leave rather than watch you drive away and get upset? Would giving her a food dispensing toy in the morning distract her? Can you block the fence (or front windows) so she doesn't see people walk by the house?

Every house, yard, dog, and owner's routine is different. Just take some time to watch and listen to your dog, ask your neighbors what they're hearing, and then try to implement some changes.

Making a Change

Teaching Quiet

A dog's bark is like a person's speech; the goal should never be to stop all barking. Not only is that impossible but trying will cause a significant amount of frustration for you and your dog. The first step to teaching your dog not to bark so much is to teach her Quiet.

Redirect Your Barking Dog

In the house when your dog barks, tell her, "Sweetie, quiet!" and let her sniff a good treat. Then tell her, "Sweetie, watch me, good!" Give her the treat. It will be difficult for her to concentrate on you and continue barking at the same time.

Ask Friends to Help

Set up a training session and have someone come ring your doorbell or pound on the door. Have your dog on leash, ask her to be quiet, and then go to the door. Interrupt her if she continues to bark.

Praise Quiet

The most effective dog trainers praise the quiet. Praise her when she's in situations where she normally barks but is quiet. Praise her when she stops barking when you ask her to. Praise her when she grumbles but isn't barking. Praise her!

Mouthing and Biting

Dogs use their mouths to manipulate their world. In dealing with the limitations of their paws, some dogs become skillful at using their jaws, teeth, and even tongue. When a dog uses her mouth on people, then problems arise.

"Mouthing" is generally defined as the dog using her mouth but not causing harm. A dog who wants her dinner and takes her owner's wrist to walk her to the kitchen is mouthing her owner. This dog may be using her mouth, but she's being gentle and not using any pressure.

A dog who is chasing the kids in the backyard, in play, and catches one of the kids by grabbing the sleeve as well as the arm is biting. She may not have shown aggression, but she used her mouth inappropriately.

Then there are dogs who bite to defend themselves, their home, or owner. Dogs who are frightened may bite. There are many situations when a dog might use her mouth, and every dog is capable of mouthing or biting given the individual circumstances.

Unfortunately, there have been far too many serious bites—each with a different story behind it, but most with tragic results. Therefore, the legal system treats dog bite cases seriously. To protect our dogs, it's important to teach them how to interact and play with humans without using their teeth.

Preventing a Problem

When playing with your dog, avoid games that teach your dog to fight you. Wrestling, finger fighting (waving your fingers in front of her face), and other games such as these aggravate your dog and basically invite her to use her mouth. Instead, play games with toys and encourage her to get and hold on to her toys as a part of the game.

Tug games can be good for some dogs as long as the dog can stop when you ask her to stop. If she gets overstimulated and can't give up the game, then this is not the right game for her.

If you dog has certain times when she is more apt to use her mouth, such as when you first come home or late at night, then at those times encourage her to grab a toy and hold on to it. Praise her for getting her toy, "Sweetie, get your toy! Good girl! Yeah!" With a toy in her mouth, her mouth is occupied.

Don't let your dog run and chase the kids when they're playing. The desire to chase and grab is far too strong. In fact, don't put her in any situations where she's apt to use her mouth. If she's going to be in one of those situations, keep her on leash and close to you so you can interrupt her before a problem occurs.

When to Get Professional Help

If your dog uses her mouth in any situation other than overzealous play, you need to talk to a professional trainer or behaviorist. If she bites guests when they come over, grabs the kids during play and breaks the skin, attempts to bite delivery men, or uses her mouth inappropriately in any other manner, you need help.

A dog who bites is a liability in many ways. Obviously you don't want other people to be hurt by your dog, nor do you want your dog destroyed because she's biting. But the ethical, legal, and financial liabilities are also huge.

To find a trainer or behaviorist in your area who is knowledgeable about working with dogs who bite, talk to several veterinarians and ask who they recommend.

Digging

Digging is another problem behavior that is a natural action for dogs. Dogs dig to hunt for gophers or moles. They dig when they hear water running in the buried sprinkler system pipes.

Dogs also dig to bury bones or toys, especially treasured ones. If your dog has played with a toy or chewed on a bone and is finished with it for the moment but doesn't want anyone else to have it, she'll find a place to bury it. Unfortunately you might not like that place because it's usually somewhere with soft dirt, like your potted plants.

Escape artists might dig to get out under the fence or gate. These dogs are not digging to find or bury something, the digging is just a part of their escape efforts.

Dogs also dig to create a place to be comfortable outside. That means in the heat of summer she'll dig a hole in the shade where she can then relax in cool dirt. In the winter, she'll find a sheltered place and dig until she finds warmer dirt.

Some dogs are more prone to major digging projects than others, and these can create huge holes in the backyard. If you have a nicely landscaped yard or if your dog creates huge or numerous holes, digging is a problem.

Preventing a Problem

Preventing digging is tough, primarily because there are so many reasons why dogs dig. It's important to watch your dog, take a look at her holes, and see if you can figure out why she was digging. Then you can address the problem.

If she's digging after critters in the yard then getting rid of the critters is certainly one step in solving the problem. That's easier said than done in many cases, but increasing your dog's exercise can often help. If your dog is tired before she goes out in the yard, she'll be less likely to dig.

A dog run with fencing on the bottom is also an option. If there is a part of the yard where you can build a secure, sheltered dog run you can put fencing across the bottom so your dog can't dig there. When your dog is outside but unsupervised, leave her in the dog run. If it won't hurt anything, you might also just let her dig to her heart's content in the dog run.

Training is rarely effective in stopping digging; it's such a natural behavior and there are so many reasons why dogs do it. Plus, your dog probably doesn't dig while you're watching her; she does it when she's alone. Corrections after the fact don't work.

A Place to Dig

If you have a dedicated digger and she takes a lot of joy in digging, you might just want to create a spot where she can do it. Once you teach her to dig there and not elsewhere, the digging won't be a problem.

Find a spot out of the way where no one will trip over the holes. Dig up a spot large enough for her to have fun with and large enough for her to lay in when she wants to—think of a sandbox area. Turn the dirt over well and break up the clumps.

Grab a handful of her toys and some dog treats and position them in this dirt. Half bury the toys and sprinkle the treats around.

Call her over and encourage her to find them, "Sweetie, where are your toys? Find them!" Point to the goodies, flip over some of the dirt, and praise her when she investigates. If she starts to dig, really praise her.

Over a couple of weeks, keep placing toys and treats in her area and taking her there. Praise her and reassure her that digging here is fun. If you catch her in the act of digging elsewhere, interrupt her, "Ack! Not there!" and take her over to her spot and encourage her again.

Destructive Chewing in the House

Dogs chew for many reasons. It usually begins when a stuffed toy is chewed on or stretched in play and the dog discovers that she can pull out the fiberfill inside. When she has fun doing that— after all spreading filling all over the place is great fun—she will be more apt to do it again later. Pretty soon every stuffed toy is quickly disemboweled. Then she may discover the sofa cushions also have stuffing.

Dogs also like to chew things that smell strongly of their owners. TV remote controls, eyeglasses, hearing aids, socks, shoes, slippers, underwear, and cell phones are all items that carry a lot of our scent because we touch them often.

Unfortunately destructive chewing is exactly that—destructive. Replacing chewed items can be expensive—especially when we're talking about eyeglasses, hearing aids, and cell phones. But even getting new sofa cushions that match the sofa isn't cheap.

Destructive chewing is also dangerous to the dog. Far too many dogs have had potentially dangerous and expensive surgery because they have eaten items that shouldn't have been eaten. Some things can pass through the digestive tract, but socks can cause obstructions and need to be removed surgically. Batteries or sharp objects will cause significant harm and often require life-saving emergency surgery.

Preventing a Problem

Destructive chewing can be caused by boredom, a lack of exercise, too much energy, or a lack of household rules. If you can figure out when and why the destruction is happening, then you can work to prevent it.

Increasing your dog's exercise and making sure she's tired whenever you leave the house is good. Making sure your dog is not eating a food high in cereal grains will reduce the chance of her suffering from a food-related hyperactivity.

Practice your obedience training. Increasing her attention to you and making training fun yet also setting some household rules is never a bad idea. Teaching the Leave It with some of the items she's prone to pay attention to is also important.

Make sure everyone in the household puts away everything they aren't using. Shoes and socks kicked off in the living room and left on the floor are an invitation for your dog to play with them. The less things are left out for your dog to grab, the fewer things get destroyed.

If your dog is a dedicated destroyer, you'll also need to make sure she's confined when in the house and unsupervised. She can be crated or in an exercise pen, or in a safe place outside; whatever works for your family, dog, and household routine.

When she has freedom of the house with family members, she needs to be supervised. Then, if she picks up something she shouldn't have, the Leave It command can be used. She can be encouraged to pick up one of her toys instead and praised for getting the toy.

Destructive Behavior Outside

Destructive behaviors outside are much like those in the house, except there is less emphasis on your possessions.

Items destroyed outside tend to be ones the dog has access to, rather than those touched often by you. Some commonly destroyed things are garden tools, children's toys, spa covers, outside wiring (including the cable), and lawn furniture. The cushions on the lawn furniture are often shredded.

Some dogs have been known to chew on the wooden deck, the picnic table, the fence, and anything else they can get their jaws around. A large breed dog with strong jaws can do an amazing amount of damage.

Dogs also like to uproot potted plants, chew on shrubs, and even destroy small trees. It's not that your dog dislikes landscaping; it's just that the plants are there.

As with chewing inside, the cost of the damage caused by a destructive dog can be horrifying. Having your house rewired for cable because the dog chewed the lines is not fun. Replacing the spa cover two or three times is expensive. In addition, if you enjoy spending time outside in your back yard when the weather is nice, that enjoyment will be lessened significantly if your dog is destructive.

Your dog can also hurt herself. Chewing electrical cables is dangerous, as is chewing—and potentially swallowing—foreign objects. Even chewing on wood is bad. Your dog could get splinters in her mouth and throat, and might need surgery if she swallows pieces of wood. Destructive chewing is bad news all the way around.

Preventing the Problem

Exercise is the first step to eliminating this problem. The vast majority of destruction happens as the owner is leaving home, so if you can provide your dog with some strenuous exercise before you leave, you could stave off some destruction.

Boredom is also a big factor. Use environmental enrichment or food dispensing toys to help keep your dog occupied. Feed her breakfast in food dispensing toys.

In hot weather, freeze food and toys in a bucket of water; you can use apple slices, chunks of carrots, some pieces of kibble, or a tennis ball. When frozen solid, remove the bucket. Let your dog work at this treasure throughout the day.

Practice your training, too, and teach your dog to ignore specific items. If she likes to chew on the lawn furniture, teach the Leave It using those as distractions.

Put things away. Until your dog is yard safe, put away everything you can. She can't chew on it if it isn't available.

For hard-core destructive dogs, build a dog run. Leave her some hard-to-destroy toys and unspillable water and, when she can't be supervised, leave her in the dog run.

Dashing Out Doors and Gates

Dogs have no sense of personal safety and don't understand that dashing out the front door or gate could have tragic consequences. Running out the door and into the street could result in the dog being hit by a car or becoming lost. She could also scare someone walking by on the sidewalk in front of the house.

Dogs dash for several reasons. If you're outside, your dog is going to want to join you—and if the door or gate is ajar, she'll push her way out. If there's a dog or person out front, she may jump at the door or gate, hoping to open it, so she can confront that dog or person.

Delivery drivers also cause an upset. Because your dog barks at these trucks and then the trucks drive away, the dog always wins. She's brave and victorious and has chased away that truck. This is reinforced each time the truck comes down your street, so if one day the door or gate is not fastened tightly, she'll be out in a flash.

This is an obviously dangerous behavior problem that needs to be addressed right away.

Prevent the Problem

Preventing the problem is relatively easy. The first thing to do is keep all doors and gates securely latched or locked. If a latch or lock is not working well, replace it.

When doors are opened, hold the dog by the collar or put a leash on her to prevent her from dashing. Or, if you have to bring in groceries or carry in an armful of something, put the dog in another room and close that door.

Ultimately, however, the best prevention is to teach the dog that she cannot dash out open doors and gates. Take your time practicing these skills and repeat them day after day, at different doors and gates. Don't assume your dog understands this for quite a while—dashing outside is a self-rewarding behavior.

Use Training to Make a Change

Leash on Dog

Have a leash hooked to your dog's collar. (Don't use a head halter here; your dog could wrench her neck.) Hold on to the leash. Choose a door your dog likes to dash out, and walk up to that door inside the house. Don't say anything to your dog.

Sit and Open Door

Have your dog sit right in front of the door, making sure there is room for the door to open if it swings inward. Praise her for sitting. Hold the leash in one hand. Open the door with the other hand and do not block the doorway.

If She Dashes Out

If your dog dashes out the door, be an anchor, and use the leash to stop her. At the same time, tell her, "Ack!" to let her know she made a mistake. Then use the leash to bring her back to the spot she vacated and have her sit again. There is no praise for coming back in or sitting.

Praise for Holding the Sit

If your dog did not dash out the open door, close it. Then go back to your dog, praise her in the sitting position, and release her. Then praise her some more. Let her know that holding that Sit in front of the open door is wonderful.

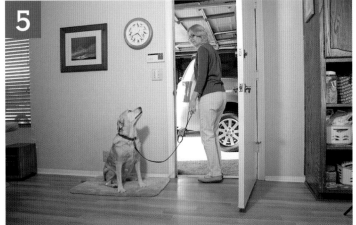

Step Out the Door

Repeat the exercise until your dog doesn't dash out when the door is opened. Then, as you hold the leash, step out the door. If your dog dashes, bring her back as you did in step 3. If your dog holds her position, go back and praise her as in step 4.

Repeat Elsewhere

Once your dog will hold her Sit as you step in and out of that door, move your practice to different doors and gates. Then, when you want her to go through the door or gate, have her on leash and give her permission, "Sweetie, okay, let's go!" And praise her.

Do You Need Professional Help?

You can do quite a bit of training on your own, but behavior problems can be tough. After all, behavior problems are not problems for your dog; she's doing these things because they are natural behaviors for her.

So, if you've been doing the obedience training and following the instructions for solving a behavior problem (or two) and you're not having any success, then it's time to call for help.

This doesn't mean you're a failure or that your dog is bad. Every dog is an individual influenced by her genetics and experiences. Some dogs will have more trouble with certain issues than others. The guardian breeds—rottweilers, mastiffs, and Great Pyrenees, for example—are going to be more protective than many other breeds. Terriers love to dig holes. Many smaller breeds tend to bark a lot. A professional trainer can help you succeed.

Take Aggression Seriously

Treat aggression very seriously, whether toward people, other dogs, or other animals. Although most dogs are protective to some degree about their property or people, most will stop or back down when asked to. Plus, many will bark but not do anything else.

However, the situation is very serious if your dog is snapping, attempting to bite, or has bitten a person. If your dog has attacked another dog or if you feel that she will if she has a chance, this, too, is serious. You will also need to seek help if your dog has attempted to attack another domestic animal.

Aggression is difficult to change, but a professional trainer or behaviorist might be able to provide you with skills to help your dog control herself as well as teach you how to keep your dog and everyone else safe.

Until you get some help, prevent your dog from causing any additional harm. Do not try to solve aggression issues yourself. The stakes are too high.

Finding a Professional

The best way to find a professional dog trainer or behaviorist in your local area is to talk to several veterinarians. They learn about other pet professionals from their clients and hear who has been successful and who hasn't. They have probably also talked to that professional and have based an opinion upon those discussions.

If you talk to several veterinarians and one or two names keep popping up, then call and talk to those people. Ask questions about their education, certifications, and whether or not they deal with aggression issues. Then choose the person who sounds right for you and your dog and make an appointment.

Dog trainers teach obedience training, although most also work with behavior problems. A veterinary behaviorist is a veterinarian with a specialty in behavior. A behavior consultant is not a veterinarian but is usually a trainer who has specialized in behavior.

Chapter 17

Trick Training and Games

- Scenting games are easy
- Trick training is mentally stimulating
- Engage with retrieving and tug games

Obedience training, problem prevention, and problem solving tend to be serious. After all, a dog can create havoc in our lives if bad behavior is allowed to continue. But you added a dog to your family for companionship, exercise, and fun.

Fun and play are important for both you and your dog. Not only does having fun together help cement that bond the two of you share, but it will also help with your training and problem prevention. You and your dog should play, have fun, and enjoy your time together.

If you're both having fun while training, the cooperation will be better and you'll both look forward to the training sessions. Your dog will be more motivated to pay attention to you and to try to do what you want him to do.

There are many ways to have fun with your dog. Retrieving games and long walks in different locations can be fun. A camping trip to the forest or the beach is exciting and a break from the normal routine. You can play brain games. Scenting games and trick training are also great fun. No matter what you decide to do, just remember you both should enjoy the activity.

Create a Brain Game at Home

One of the easiest—and most fun—brain games that you can create at home is the muffin tin game. This game requires your dog to use his scenting abilities to do some problem solving. He needs to think about what he's doing and remember what he's already done.

Your job is to show him what's involved and then to be a cheerleader. In the beginning, he's not going to know what to do or why; your encouragement will keep him working at it.

For this game, your dog will need to find some good treats that are placed in the holes of the muffin tin and then covered by tennis balls. The tennis balls fit perfectly in the holes; your dog will need to either lift them out or paw hard to dislodge them.

Sometimes a dislodged ball will land in a hole that was already searched. He'll need to remember which holes he's searched and which he hasn't. Of course he should also be able to smell whether a treat remains in the hole, or was once there and now is gone.

Dogs play this in various ways. Some are slow and studious, carefully sniffing each hole and moving one ball at a time. Some dogs are more excited and bounce all around the muffin tin, sniffing here and there, and dislodging random balls. And then some dogs are impatient. An Australian shepherd picked up the muffin tin by the edge and flipped it over, sending balls and treats every which way.

The Muffin Tin Game

Set Up the Game

Have your game parts at hand: 12-hole muffin tin, 12 tennis balls, and some good treats. For this game the best treats are ones with a strong scent. Swiss cheese works great. Place a treat in every hole of the tin, then cover each hole with a tennis ball.

Place Tin on Floor

Place the muffin tin on the floor and encourage your dog to investigate it. Let him sniff it all over, touch it, and even paw it. You can slightly lift a ball so he can see and smell the treat underneath but then drop the ball. When he picks up or nudges a ball, praise him.

Encourage Your Dog

One of the benefits of this game is that your dog learns to solve a problem. The treats are under the ball so he needs to figure out how to get them. Help him and encourage him, but let him think.

Reload and Do It Again

Once you've helped your dog complete the first game, reload it and do it again. Depending on your dog, you may want to use a different treat this time. You can also continue to help your dog or, if your dog did well on the first game, back off just a little this time.

A Fun Scenting Game

For most dogs, the sense of smell is much more important than other senses. There are some breeds that don't use their sense of smell as well—pugs and bulldogs are two—because the physical structure of their nose and nasal passages makes it hard. But for most dogs, the nose tells them the most about their world. You can use your dog's scenting abilities to play some games that he'll really enjoy.

Scenting games can be played outside or moved inside when the weather is bad. Although your dog's body is not getting exercised, his brain sure is and that's always good.

Choose a good treat to be used as bait for the games. The treat needs to be something your dog really likes and it should have a good scent. Your dog is going to be searching for this treat, so it will serve as both the bait and the reward.

Later, when your dog knows the game well, you can change what he's searching for. It can be his favorite tennis ball, or even a totally different scent such as a piece of cotton scented with an oil like lavender, anise, or birch. To start, however, you'll use a treat.

Bring Out the Boxes

Set Out Some Boxes
With your dog in a Sit and Stay, scatter several boxes on the ground a few steps in front of him. The boxes should be a variety of sizes, new and used, and of different kinds. They can be open, semi-open, and one or two can be closed.

"Sweetie, find it!"
Drop some treats in two or three of the boxes. Then go back to your dog, release him, and tell him, "Sweetie, find it!" Encourage him to move toward the boxes. You need to encourage him but let him learn to search.

Reward Liberally
When your dog finds a treat in a box, drop some more in so he gets a jackpot reward. Praise him, "Sweetie, you are awesome! Yeah." Then, encourage him to keep searching. You can take one step toward the next treat box, but don't guide him; let him search.

Keep Searching
Once your dog has found all of the treats, then ask him to sit and stay while you rearrange the boxes and reload them with treats. Two or three searches are good for one session.

More Scenting Games

Once your dog understands scenting games, there are many different ways you can play because the basic premise is always the same: follow your nose. When your dog is proficient at finding the treats in boxes, then substitute something else for the boxes.

You can hide the treats in paper cups and fold one edge over once the treat is inside. Or you can use empty paper towel and toilet paper cardboard tubes, again with one edge of each end folded over once the treat is inside. The folded edge helps keep the treat inside as you set up the game.

One game that's lots of fun (and great to show off to friends) is based on a carnival chance game. At a carnival, the game operator will have three inverted cups and he'll place a ping pong ball under one of them. Then he'll move the cups around and around, trying to confuse you. You'll have to guess where the ball is.

You can do this with your dog and I bet your dog will win almost every time. Once he knows the game, he'll probably win every time. To play you'll need three small plastic flower pots and some treats.

The Flower Pot Game

Sit on the floor with your dog. Invert the flower pots and let your dog watch as you place a treat under one of them. Then tell your dog, "Sweetie, find it!" as he sniffs the pots, encourage him. When he sniffs hard at the pot with the treat and gives you a sign that he knows the treat is there—staring at you or pawing the pot—praise him and tip the pot over. Let him have the treat.

After he's played this a few times, wait a bit to reward him and see if he will knock the pot over himself. Some dogs will do it with a paw and others will flip it with their nose. Praise him when he does it.

Three to four repetitions of this game are enough for one session. Remember he's using his brain here as well as his nose and you don't want him to get frustrated or bored.

After several days of playing the game, when your dog is finding the treat reliably, then you can make it more difficult. Once you hide the treat, move the pots around a few times. Then encourage your dog to search. When he finds the treat, really praise him.

The Plastic Egg Game

This game uses plastic eggs sold around Easter. Choose the larger-size plastic eggs—you don't want your dog to grab one and swallow it.

Gather several dozen plastic eggs and put some smelly treats in about six of them. Scatter all of the eggs on the living room floor or outside on the ground. Tell your dog to find it.

To get the treat he has to show you that he knows a treat is inside, so you need to watch his body language. How is he communicating that knowledge to you? Some dogs will paw the eggs while some will sniff it so hard they sound like a vacuum cleaner.

When your dog has found an egg with a treat, pick up the egg, open it, and let your dog get the treat out of the egg. Praise him.

Tricks are Training and Fun

Trick training is a special kind of training. Not only are you still teaching your dog—it's also great fun. You can giggle as you teach your dog, laugh with him when he makes mistakes, and cheer him on when he does it right. It's all fun, and that's what dog training should be.

Trick training is particularly useful for dogs (or owners) who get bogged down when teaching the basic obedience exercises. If you feel like the basic obedience isn't fun or if you simply get bored teaching it to your dog, then intersperse some trick training with the basic exercises.

Therapy dogs can always use some tricks in their volunteer work. Tricks are a great conversation starter when visiting people; especially when introducing yourself and your dog to someone new. Tricks also make people laugh.

The tricks in this section will be taught using the lure and reward technique. Each trick is broken down into steps here. However, if your dog is having trouble or is confused, feel free to break it into even smaller steps. Smaller steps, practiced often, and reinforced with praise and treats, can cut through that confusion.

Use good treats or a favorite toy as both a lure and a reward. Vary the treats or toy to keep your dog's enthusiasm high. Then keep training sessions short, especially in the beginning. Remember, when you first started teaching the obedience exercises, your dog didn't understand why things were changing. The same can happen with trick training.

Teach Shake Then Wave

Setting Up the Shake

Have your dog sit in front of you. He can be on leash if you think he might dash away; however, since you're going to need both hands, drop the leash to the ground and step on it. Have some treats in your left hand. You're going to be shaking with your right.

Tickle and Shake

Reach with your right hand and tickle the little hollow spot behind your dog's paw. When he begins to lift his paw, tell him, "Sweetie, shake!" Pop a treat in his mouth as you gently place your right hand under that slightly lifted paw. Do not grasp his paw; just place your hand under it.

Paw in Hand

Continue tickling behind the paw until your dog is lifting his paw as you reach toward him. Praise that enthusiastically! Then simply ask him to shake (without a tickle) and place your hand under his paw. Then begin praising more when he lifts his paw higher, creating a better shake.

The Wave

When your dog is shaking well, then you can also teach him to wave. Reach toward his paw without saying shake. He'll recognize the hand movement and lift his paw. Reach toward him as if to shake but hold your hand higher. When he reaches higher toward your hand, tell him, "Sweetie, wave! Good!"

Peek-a-Boo

Getting Ready

In this trick, your dog is going to move from in front of you, around your right leg, and then come from the back between your legs, and stop with her head between your legs facing forward. Your dog will need to be off leash. Begin by standing in front of your dog with a treat in each hand.

Lead Your Dog to the Right

Let your dog sniff the treat in your right hand. Encourage her to follow your hand and move her slowly toward your right side. If she stops after a step or two, that's fine, praise her and give her the treat. Practice this until she will walk from in front of you to your right side and around your right leg.

The Left Hand Goes Back

When your right hand has brought your dog around your right leg to behind you, pull your right hand up to your body away from your dog. At the same time—and this requires some coordination—put your left hand between your legs so your dog can sniff that treat. You want to catch your dog before he goes all the way around you.

Bring Dog Forward Between Legs

With your left hand between your legs, let your dog sniff the treat. Then lead your dog forward between your legs. When his head is in front of your legs and the rest of him is behind you, tell him, "Sweetie, peek-a-boo! Good!" and pop the treat in his mouth. Release him and praise him.

Spin Right and Left

Spin Right

Let your dog sniff a really good treat in your right hand. Once he smells it, then begin moving your hand—and your dog—in a circle to the right. As he's moving, tell him, "Sweetie, spin right!" If he stops partway around, that's okay. Praise him and give him the treat. After several attempts, he'll go all the way around and you can reward him for that.

Minimize Signal

As you practice this trick, over time and many training sessions, begin minimizing the hand motion. Instead of using a big signal in front of your dog's nose, decrease the circle and hand signal until you can make a small circular motion to the right. Use lots of positive reinforcements—especially praise—as you do this.

Spin Left
When your dog is spinning to the right well and you've been able to minimize the hand signal, then start teaching your dog to spin to the left. Go back to the first step; treat in front of the nose and lead him to the left in a circle, "Sweetie, spin left." Be prepared for some confusion because he thinks he's supposed to move to the right.

Spin Quickly
Take your time teaching spin left to your dog so you can keep his confusion under control. If he stops, don't worry about it—just help him. When he's learned it, then decrease the hand signal as you did for spin right. Then challenge him. Have him spin right, then spin left, then right again. Be sure to stop before he's dizzy.

Weave the Legs

Setting up the Weave

For this trick your dog will weave a figure eight pattern around your legs. Begin with your dog standing in front of you, facing you. Have some treats in each hand. Stand with your legs about shoulder-width apart. If you have a small dog your legs can be closer together; for a large dog, farther apart.

From Front to Back Right

With your right hand, reach around your right leg so your dog can see the treat between your legs. If he needs help, use your left hand to guide your dog toward your right hand. As your dog moves between your legs tell him, "Sweetie, weave." Bring your dog back toward the front, curving him around your right leg. Praise him as he's moving.

From Front to Back Left

Your dog should now be coming to the front of you, curved around your right leg. With your left hand, get his attention and pull him again between your legs toward the back. Then curve him around behind your left leg. As you do this, repeat the verbal cue, "Sweetie, weave!" Praise him.

From the Left to the Front

With your left hand, bring your dog around your left leg to the front so he completes the figure eight around your legs. Praise and pet him, "Sweetie, yeah! Awesome!" As you practice and your dog moves more smoothly through the figure eight, you can decrease some of the movements.

Just Play

Play is a wonderful thing. Not only will playing with your dog help you bond with him and cement your relationship, but playing with him can make training fun.

Play is a natural behavior that most species engage in. Young mammals in particular love to play. Even fish have been known to play, usually with items in their environment—although it's hard for us to understand what a fish is thinking, we can understand play when we see it.

Puppies are wonderful examples of the benefits of play. Play is exercise; it's bonding and relationship building; it makes us happy—there is nothing better than that.

It's imperative that you take time to play with your dog. What kind of games you play are up to you and your dog. If you're not in the habit of playing, perhaps in the beginning you need to schedule the time to do it.

Eventually you'll be able to be more spontaneous. Lean over, pat your knees with your hands, and smile at your dog. (This is the human version of a canine play bow—an invitation to play.) Then dash away. I'll bet your dog follows you! Then turn around bow again, and see what your dog does. Imitate each other, laugh, and enjoy yourself.

Retrieving Games

These can be played with flying discs, tennis balls, or any other ball or toy that can be thrown and is safe for your dog to catch. Although many puppies are too distracted by life in general to retrieve a thrown toy all the time, many adult dogs enjoy chasing, retrieving, and bringing back toys.

If your dog is not into retrieving, start with very short tosses—just a couple of feet—and really encourage your dog to chase the toy. Praise him and make a big fuss over his efforts.

If your dog doesn't like to give toys back, trade him a treat for the toy. As he drops the toy, tell him, "Sweetie, give!" and pop the treat in his mouth.

Tug Games

Tug games, often called tug-of-war games, used to be discouraged by dog trainers. They were thought to be too rough or too aggressive. Although tug games can be played with most dogs, they are too stimulating for some dogs.

The first rule of tug games is that you get to stop the game. If you're playing tug with your dog and you've had enough, you should be able to tell your dog to give you the toy and he should do it without a fuss.

Also, if your dog gets so stimulated by the game that he keeps grabbing the toy—working closer and closer to your hands—and you're worried about him grabbing you, then this isn't the right game. If you don't experience any of these problems, tug games are great. Dogs love them, they use a lot of energy, and they're fun.

Games to Avoid

Don't play any games that teach your dog to fight you. Wrestling is not recommended. For example, if you routinely wrestle with your dog, rolling around on the floor, pinning him and letting him jump on you, then what happens if you need to take care of his body? Perhaps you need to roll him over to clean a cut (or surgical incision) on the inside of a leg or on his belly. Rolling him over means time to fight you, right?

Don't let him do anything while playing that you won't allow him to do at other times. If he's not normally allowed on the sofa, don't let him jump on it and bounce off the back of it during play. He's not going to understand the difference, so it's up to you to remain consistent.

If your dog becomes overstimulated while you're playing, stop the game. Walk away; leave him outside while you go in—or vice versa. If that isn't enough, he can have a time-out in his crate. He needs to know the game is over if he gets too rough.

Chapter 18

Canine Sports and Activities

- The benefits of CGC
- Show off your skills with Rally
- Agility is great fun
- Therapy dogs provide affection

Once you and your dog are proficient with the basic obedience skills, there is a whole new world for you to explore. The range of dog activities and sports is huge. Your involvement can be simple—such as fund-raising walks for dogs and owners to support dog rescue or veterinary efforts—to more complicated sports that require a great deal of training. You can choose depending on your likes and dislikes, the time you have available, and your dog's abilities.

The American Kennel Club's Canine Good Citizen program is often the first step for dogs and owners. The goal of this program is to promote responsible dog ownership and the joys of a well-trained dog. Often the only times dogs are highlighted in the media is when there has been a horrible dog bite incident. While those situations are terrible, there are far more nice dogs than horrible ones, and the Canine Good Citizen program promotes those good dogs.

Rally provides dogs and their owners a way to continue practicing their obedience skills and to compete as well. Though dogs can earn titles while competing, Rally is still informal and friendly, and other competitors are supportive of each other. This is a fun sport.

Agility is both fun and competitive. It's also quite amazing. When you watch dogs competing off leash, following their owners' directions to go from obstacle to obstacle around a timed course, you'll be in awe of the relationship and teamwork between dog and owner.

There is much more: an alphabet of activities from agility to weight pulling. What you decide to get involved in depends on you and your dog. No matter what activity you choose, make sure you both enjoy it.

The Canine Good Citizen Program

In the 1980s and 1990s, dogs were being portrayed badly in the media. Whereas previously dogs were seen as mankind's best friends, now they were trouble. Dog bites made the headlines and many cities listed barking dogs as one of the most numerous complaints they received from their residents. The pit bull hysteria was growing. It was becoming a tough time to be a dog owner (or a dog).

The American Kennel Club (AKC) introduced the Canine Good Citizen (CGC) Program in 1989. One of the goals of the program then and now is to promote (and publicize) responsible dog ownership. This includes training, providing veterinary care, and good grooming. The CGC also seeks to recognize well-behaved dogs, not just at home but also out in public.

The CGC is open to all dogs—purebreds and mixed breeds, those registered with the AKC and those that are not. The program's developers realized that it was for everyone's benefit to encourage good dogs of all breeds and mixtures of breeds.

The CGC Test

Tests are given in a wide variety of places. Dog shows often include the CGC. Kennel clubs, dog training clubs, dog trainers, and special events for dogs all often include the CGC test.

The test consists of ten exercises. The dog and owner must pass all ten parts. If the dog doesn't pass, you retake the test after your dog has had more practice.

- Test 1: Accepting a friendly stranger. Your dog will sit by your side and remain there while someone comes up to greet you.

- Test 2: Sitting politely for petting. When greeted by a friendly person, your dog will sit nicely for petting.

- Test 3: Appearance and grooming. Your dog is healthy and well groomed, and will accept someone touching her and briefly brushing her.

- Test 4: Out for a walk on a loose leash. Your dog is paying attention to you and will walk nicely with you without pulling.

- Test 5: Walk with distractions. The dog will walk nicely with you while walking through a crowd of people (at least three).

- Test 6: Sit, Down, and Stay. The dog must demonstrate that she can do a Sit, Down, and Stay. The Stay can be either a Sit Stay or a Down Stay.

- Test 7: Come when called. The dog will come to you when you call her from ten feet away. She will be on a long leash.

- Test 8: Reaction to another dog. One dog and owner will approach another dog and owner. The dogs will sit next to their owners and ignore or show no more than casual interest in each other.

- Test 9: Reaction to distractions. This shows that your dog will not panic or overreact to everyday distractions, including sights and sounds.

- Test 10: Supervised separation. A trusted person will remain with your dog while you go out of sight for three minutes.

Finding a CGC Test

To find a CGC test, call several dog trainers or dog training clubs in your area. Many probably hold CGC tests several times during the year.

Some trainers also hold CGC classes. Although a class isn't always necessary to pass the test, the classes can be useful as they are usually designed around the various exercises. Not only does this instruction help you understand the goal of each exercise but you get a chance to practice it, too.

You can also check the AKC website where a list of CGC evaluators is posted. You can search for evaluators in your area.

Introducing Rally

Rally is a sport based on obedience training. The dog and owner proceed around a course, with the dog in the heel position, going from card to card. Each card contains instructions for the dog and owner to perform. When that activity is completed, they move on to the next one.

The appeal of Rally to many obedience competitors is that it is a little more informal and friendly. Whereas in competitive obedience, the owner can only give commands to her dog and cannot help her in the competition, in Rally you can talk to your dog and encourage her.

Rally competitions are available through many different organizations, including the American Kennel Club, the United Kennel Club, and the Association of Pet Dog Trainers. There are even programs offered by the Swedish Working Dog Association and the CSEN Rally-Obedience program in Italy.

AKC Rally Competition

Rally can be either competitive or noncompetitive—for keeping your obedience training interesting. Each of the organizations is slightly different, with their own rules, regulations, and titles.

AKC Rally has three levels of competition:

- Novice: The dog will be on leash. There will be between 10 and 15 cards (or stations) for the dog to perform. After 3 qualifying runs, the title earned is Rally Novice (RN).
- Advanced: This is open to dogs who have earned the RN title. The dog will work off leash. After 3 qualifying runs, the title earned is Rally Advanced (RA).
- Excellent: This is open to dogs who have earned their RA title. The dog is again working off leash and will work through 15 to 20 cards, 2 of which are jumps. After 3 qualifying runs, the title earned is Rally Excellent (RE).

Plus, there is a championship level. To earn Rally Advanced Excellent (RAE), the dog and owner must have qualifying runs in Advanced and Excellent in 10 competitions.

Rally Exercises

During a Rally competition (or training), the exercise to be performed at each station is printed on a card. This card will be set or fastened so it won't fall down or blow away, and so that it is easily read.

Some of the exercises for Rally Novice could include:

- Halt and sit.
- Right turn or left turn. Each of these is to be a 90-degree turn.
- About turn right or U-turn—which will be to the left. Each of these is to be a 180-degree turn.
- Heeling at a normal brisk pace, or slow, or fast.
- Side step right during the Heel—you will take one step to your right as you're heeling.

For Rally Advanced, any of the Novice exercises could be included as well as additional exercises. They might include:

- Halt, sit your dog, then make a 90-degree pivot to the right or left, and halt and sit your dog again.
- Halt, sit your dog, turn right one step and call your dog to the heel position.
- Halt, sit your dog, stand your dog and walk around her.

For Rally Excellent, any of the previous exercises may be used as well as additional exercises. They could include:

- Halt and sit your dog, down your dog, then sit your dog.
- Halt and sit your dog, stand your dog, then sit your dog.
- While heeling, back up three steps with your dog still heeling with you, then walk forward again.

If you and your dog enjoy training, Rally is great fun. It can be challenging, but that's good, too.

Athletic Agility

Agility is a fast-moving athletic sport in which the dog and owner move around a course predetermined by the judge, with the owner giving the dog directions as to which obstacle to do next. The dog is off leash and the owner cannot touch either the dog or the obstacle, and cannot use food treats. The owner therefore uses body language, hand signals and arm gestures, and verbal cues to guide the dog. The team is judged according to the speed of their run as well as how well they did it.

Agility can be noncompetitive or competitive for titles. When noncompetitive, dog owners generally use the obstacles as a training challenge—teaching the dog to follow directions and perform the obstacles correctly—as well as a fun way for the dog to get some exercise.

The Obstacles

Each organization that offers agility training has its own rules and list of agility obstacles. This will include the size of the obstacles as well as other construction details. Each organization will also have details regarding the height of the dogs in specific classes and what heights those dogs will need to jump.

Some of the more common obstacles include:

- **Jumps:** Jumps come in a variety of types and construction. The simplest are upright ends that support a single bar. Others may have two or three end bars that each support either parallel or ascending bars. Jumps may also have panel-type ends rather than upright ends.

- **Tire Jumps:** These consist of a frame that supports a hanging tire-type jump. The dog must jump through the tire.

- **Tunnels:** Tunnels can be straight and open so the dog can run through and while running can see the open end. The flexible tunnel can be moved so as to create a curve (or two). This tunnel is also open but the dog may not be able to see the end. Plus, a collapsed tunnel will have fabric at the end that the dog will have to push through.

- **A-frame:** This obstacle has two broad ramps fastened at the top forming a pyramid-shaped obstacle. Organizations differ regarding its size and the height at the top and whether it can have either slats or a rubberized surface to help the dogs climb it. The dogs climb up one side and down the other.

- **Dogwalk:** This looks like a balance beam for dogs except that it is made of boards from 9 to 12 inches wide. There is a ramp up, a ramp down the other side, and a horizontal board in between.

- **Weave poles:** This obstacle is something like a slalom. Upright, 3-feet-tall poles are spaced 24 inches apart and the dog must weave through the poles in a serpentine manner.

Other obstacles may include a teeter-totter (similar to one on kids' playgrounds), or a sway bridge (a ramp up, a suspended moveable bridge in the middle, and a ramp down).

Because of the variety in obstacles, check out the organizations that offer competitions in your area before you begin training. You don't want to show up at a competition and face an obstacle your dog has never seen.

Agility Competitions

Many different organizations offer agility competitions. The AKC, UKC, and Australian Shepherd Club of America offer competitions and titles, as does the United States Dog Agility Association and the North American Dog Agility Council.

During competition there are a variety of classes, depending on what is offered at any given competition, as well as the organization hosting it. Some classes may include:

- **Standard or Regular Class:** This is a numbered course in which the obstacles must be performed in order.

- **Jumpers:** This is a numbered course that consists primarily of different jumps, but some organizations will also include weave poles and/or tunnels.

- **Power and Speed:** This consists of a series of obstacles with contact zones that must be touched correctly by the dog as well as a timed section of the course made up of jumps.

These are just three of the many classes available. The various classes are designed for fun and entertainment, or to create a more challenging experience. Agility can be fun for beginning dogs and owners as well as more experienced dogs and owners.

Therapy Dogs

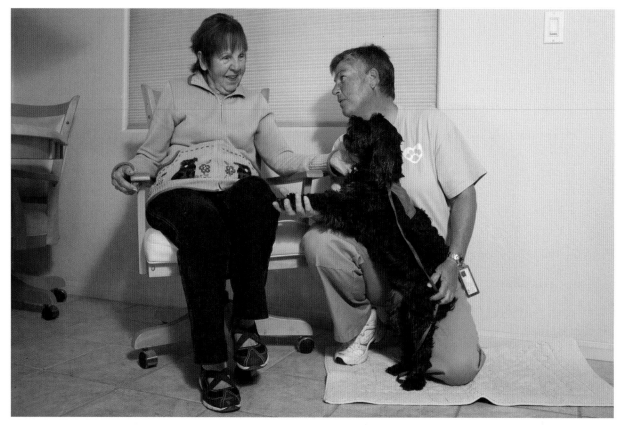

Therapy dogs visit people in hospitals, nursing homes, skilled nursing facilities, Alzheimer facilities, and a variety of other places to offer companionship, warmth, affection, and touch. The importance of this cannot be understated. Numerous studies have shown that people who do not receive this attention can fail to thrive. We need warmth and affection; we need to touch other warm bodies—be they human or canine.

This is also a team effort—both the dog and owner are vital parts of the team. The owner trains the dog, prepares the dog for visits, introduces the dog, and initiates a conversation if appropriate; the dog provides the warmth and affection.

Potential Therapy Dogs

Not all dogs can be therapy dogs. Although there are no requirements or limitations on breeds, there are some characteristics that have been shown to work better for therapy work.

- **Size:** Small dogs can be carried or lifted so people can pet them. Giant dogs can always lie down if someone is intimidated. Medium- and large-size dogs are the easiest for people to reach when the dogs are standing on the floor.

- **Coat Type:** This is entirely a matter of personal preference. The dogs do need to be clean and well groomed, with no fleas or ticks.

- **Temperament and personality:** Therapy dogs must like people. A dog who isn't fond of strangers—a fearful dog or a shy one—is not going to enjoy this work. At the same time, a dog who loves people cannot be so exuberant that she's a danger to those she's visiting.

- **Socialization:** The dog must be well socialized to people of all ages, sizes and shapes, and ethnic backgrounds.

- **Training:** All of the certifying organizations require a certain level of training and obedience. Some use the CGC test while others have their own test that is similar but uses skills needed for therapy dogs.

An ideal therapy dog can be of any breed or mix, but must be well trained and socialized, like people but have self-control around them, and be free of fleas and ticks. Of course, that dog's owner must also like people.

Therapy Dog Training

Some dog trainers offer therapy dog classes that can be beneficial, though they aren't required by most of the therapy dog organizations. Most classes introduce the dog to equipment and situations that could be encountered during visits.

Some of the skills that your dog might need include:

- Socialization to wheelchairs, walkers, and canes is important. Teaching her how to approach them from the side rather than the front can help the people she's visiting balance themselves. Plus, by introducing these pieces of equipment during training, she won't be startled on a visit.

- Teaching your small- to medium-size dog the exercise "Paws up" will enable her to place her paws on the arm of a wheelchair, the cross bar of a walker, or the side of a bed so people can reach her more readily.

- It's also good if your dog knows a command such as, "Watch your paws," so you can guide her over or around obstacles that might be in a hospital or nursing home room. Here's a hint: Put a ladder flat on the ground and ask your dog to walk the length of it, helping her step over each rung without tripping.

The most important thing about therapy dog training is that your dog enjoys the training and work. Use your training skills to keep this training effective, yet fun.

Safety Is Imperative

You and your dog will be visiting children or people who may already be ill, injured, elderly, frail, mentally impaired, or disabled in some way. It's important that everyone—including your dog—remains safe.

Some guidelines:

- Pay attention to quarantine signs. If someone is potentially contagious, the room is usually marked "restrictive access" or "quarantine." Do not visit those rooms.

- Make sure your dog does not jump up on people. This absolutely cannot happen on a visit.

- Pawing at people cannot be allowed either. The danger of scratching is too high. If it does happen, make sure you notify the staff.

- Your dog cannot use his mouth on people. Some people like kisses (licks), but ask them first. No mouthing is to be allowed, and it should go without saying that biting is never acceptable.

- Hold on to your dog's leash at all times and never leave your dog. You two are a team and the leash is an umbilical cord.

When safety is taken into consideration at all times, therapy dog work is one of the most rewarding things you can do with your dog.

There's So Much More

The dog activities and sports listed above are some of the most popular ones. But there are quite a few others that many dog owners enjoy.

Hiking, camping, and backpacking is much more fun when your dog can come with you. There are many packs available that your dog can wear so she can either carry a couple of water bottles or perhaps her own food.

Carting originated from need hundreds of years ago. At many times in our history, dogs were needed to pull carts or wagons. Perhaps the dog owner couldn't afford a horse or a horse would be too big. Dogs also pulled (and still pull) travois, milk carts, sleds, and skiers.

Schutzhund is a sport that originated in military and police dog work. Dogs competing in schutzhund are tested in many different areas, but primarily in obedience, tracking, and protection.

Tracking, air scenting, and search and rescue work all use the dog's sense of smell. Although tracking can be a competitive sport, all three activities have a practical application for finding people who are lost and/or potentially in danger.

Herding and stockdog work began on farms and ranches, but today it's also a competitive sport that uses a herding dog's natural instincts to work stock. Those instincts are combined with training to create a fun sport with practical applications.

Weight pulling contests show off how much weight a dog can pull, with the competitions broken down into size categories. Flying disc competitions recognize the dog and owner with the best routines and most catches. Field trials showcase hunting dogs' instincts and skills.

Check out some of the many activities and sports available and get to know them. Choose one or two that look like they will suit both your dog's abilities and your interests, and that you'll both have fun doing.

Glossary

agility   A sport in which the dog and owner compete; the dog completes a variety of obstacles while the owner runs with him and directs him.

behavior   Your dog's actions and patterns of actions.

Canine Good Citizen   An American Kennel Club program to acknowledge and promote responsible dog ownership and well-behaved dogs.

Come   This verbal cue tells your dog to come to you immediately with no detours.

Down   This verbal cue tells your dog to lay down on the floor or ground and not get up.

environment   Your dog's home, yard, neighborhood, and everything around him that affects his life and behavior.

Give   This verbal cue tells your dog to place the item he has in his mouth into your open hand.

Heel   This verbal cue tells your dog to walk by your left side with his shoulder next to your leg and maintain this position as you walk together.

housetraining   The process of teaching a puppy where to relieve himself.

interruption   Using a sound of some kind to interrupt an unwanted behavior as it is happening.

Leave It   This verbal cue tells your dog to ignore whatever he was paying attention to and look to you for more guidance.

leg lifting   Also known as "marking," this is when a male dog (also occasionally a female) lifts a leg to urinate on a vertical surface.

Let's Go   This verbal cue tells your dog that he can walk on the leash without heeling, as long as he doesn't pull on the leash.

lure   Something the dog likes—usually a food treat or toy—used to help him assume a position or do something you want him to do.

mark   The process of acknowledging behavior immediately—as it happens.

negative punishment   Something rewarding is removed or taken away.

negative reinforcement   Something the dog dislikes is introduced during bad behavior and then is removed when the dog's behavior changes.

personality   A dog's personality develops through life experiences.

positive punishment   Something the dog dislikes is used to decrease the frequency of a behavior.

positive reinforcement   Adding something to training that the dog likes; rewards for cooperation or behavior.

praise   Using a happy tone of voice to mark and reward good behavior.

Rally   An obedience competition sport.

Release   This verbal cue tells your dog he has finished an exercise and can move freely.

reward   Something the dog likes that is used to acknowledge good behavior; can be praise, treats, toys, or petting.

Sit   This verbal cue tells your dog to place his hips on the floor but keep his front legs upright and straight, and hold still.

socialization   The process of introducing a puppy to the world around him.

Stay   This verbal cue tells your dog to hold a position until you come back to release him.

temperament   The part of your dog's unique nature that was present at birth.

therapy training   A noncompetitive volunteer avocation where dogs and owners visit people in nursing homes and hospitals.

trick training   A fun type of training that uses training skills to teach the dog unique, fun actions.

Wait   This verbal cue tells your dog to hold still but pay attention to you because more instructions will be following soon.

Watch Me   This verbal cue tells your dog to look at your face and focus on you.

Index

Q-R

W-X-Y-Z

U-V